THE BOOK OF
CHRISTMAS FOLKLORE

THE BOOK OF
CHRISTMAS FOLKLORE

Tristram Potter Coffin

A Continuum Book

THE SEABURY PRESS · NEW YORK

ACKNOWLEDGMENTS

See pages vii–viii, which constitute an extension of this copyright page.

Copyright © 1973 by Tristram Potter Coffin.
Design by Nancy Dale Muldoon
Printed in the United States of America

LIBRARY OF CONGRESS CATALOGING IN PUBLICATION DATA

Coffin, Tristram Potter, 1922–
    The book of Christmas folklore.

    (A Continuum book)
    1. Christmas. I. Title
GT4985.C546   394.2'68282   73–6413
ISBN 0-8164-9158-5

NOWELL!

This book is dedicated to "'Ma in her 'kerchief." It is not the usual Christmas book, a petite garland for the "peace on earth, good will to men" set. But it is no gift for a Scrooge either, for a cane-tapper who refuses to have a tree, buys what presents he must in the January sales, and tosses away cards from well-wishers like bills already paid. No, it is a book for a reader not unlike the author, a fellow who awaits each Christmas with a mixture of tenderness, charity, surfeit, and astonishment, who would miss the Day were it to vanish, but who wants to learn what he can about it—willy-nilly. A book, Oscar Wilde might say, for the chap who cares to know not only the value, but also the price, of a wonder-filled tradition.

ACKNOWLEDGMENTS

LIKE all authors, I recognize sources, permissions, and kindnesses that I could not have done without. I wish to acknowledge them here, sincerely—and the acknowledgment includes those various, brief passages quoted in "fair use." I went to the pages of the *Journal of American Folklore* for a number of selections which are reprinted with permission: the Chichicastenango tale (1949, 125 f.), the description of the Guilford County, North Carolina, Christmas (1917, 208), the John Kuners passage from Dougald MacMillan's article (1926, 54–55), the cast from the Kentucky mountain drama (1938, 10), the passages from John Bourke (1893, 89 f.), the recollection of mumming in Belfast (1918, 168–169), and the quotation from Charles Welch, on the Philadelphia Mummers' Parade (1966, 523). I have also used with permission of the University of Toronto Press a short quotation from pp. 84–85 of Herbert Halpert and G. M. Story (eds.), *Christmas Mumming in Newfoundland,* 1969, Copyright Canada 1969 by University of Toronto Press. The descriptions of mumming in Norfolk, Fife, and Dorset are from C. H. Stephenson, *Notes and Queries,* Fourth Series, VIII, 525; J. A. Brown, *The Golden Days of Youth,* 1893, 121; and Marianne R. Dacombe, *Dorset Up Along and Down Along,* 1936, 103 respectively. They also appear in Halpert and Story. The translations of Libanius, the Priest of Cronus, Ethelwold of Winchester, and Caesarius of Arles were made with assistance from those in E. K. Chambers, *The Medieval*

Stage, 2 vols., Oxford, 1903, 54, while the recipe for boar's head is developed from the one printed in William Seymour and John Smith, *Happy Christmas*, 1968, 87. The Dingley Dell mistletoe scene is from Chapter 28 of Dickens' *The Pickwick Papers*, and there are two brief quotations in Chapter 1 from William Prynne's *Histrio-mastix*. The press clipping by Robert Musel quoted on page 137 is reprinted with permission of United Press International (formerly United Press Associations). All other references are given in passing in the text.

Persons who have helped here and there along the way include: Allen Chester, Robert Evans, Paul Lloyd, Robert Lumiansky, and Craig Thompson—all of the University of Pennsylvania faculty. I am also particularly indebted to my son, Mark T. Coffin, who did some of the research for Chapter 4, and to my daughter, Priscilla R. Coffin, who typed the manuscript and helped with the indexing and proofreading.

Finally, let me acknowledge that any originality in a book such as this depends on arrangement and commentary, not on the selections reproduced. I am aware that many of the latter have been printed a number of times before. I am also aware that, on the whole, I have confined myself to Anglo-American tradition.

CONTENTS

THE BOOK OF
CHRISTMAS FOLKLORE

1

CHRISTMAS AULD LANG SYNE

MOST of us, if we think about it at all, have a vague idea that the celebration of Christmas began on December 25, the year Zero, when a Star rose in the East and a Saviour was born. Of course, such was hardly the case. The celebration of Christmas really began "circa 320 A.D." when the Catholic fathers in Rome decided to convert the Mithraic "Birthday of the Unconquered Sun" into a birthday more suited to their aims. Western Christians had long harbored a belief that the day involved, the twenty-fifth, was the date on which Mary bore her Son, but they hadn't been able to settle on the month. For over three centuries they had no agreed-upon time for the commemoration, and in many places it came during the feast of the Epiphany, January 6, when Jesus was supposed to have manifested Himself to the Magi and so to the Gentiles. What's more, the Eastern half of the Church had not gone along, preferring a "movable date" which they fixed by means of the moon and which they observed for nearly a century. Even after matters were stabilized on December 25, there was little pretense that the date was historically accurate. Its appeal lay in

3

definitude and its ability to align Roman ritualism with "the cause."

The "Birthday of the Unconquered Sun" was preceded in Rome by a seven-day tribute to the God of Agriculture, Saturn, and followed by the Kalends of January. Descriptions and reports of these festivities ring familiar to modern ears. Libanius, a fourth-century Greek, writes that:

The festival of the Kalends is celebrated everywhere as far as the limits of the Roman Empire extend ... Everywhere may be seen carousals and well-laden tables; luxurious abundance is found in the houses of the rich, but also in the houses of the poor; better food than usual is put upon the table. The impulse to spend seizes everyone. He who erstwhile was accustomed and preferred to live poorly, now at this feast enjoys himself as much as his means will allow. . . . People are not only generous towards themselves, but also towards their fellow-men. A stream of presents pours itself out on all sides. . . . The highroads and footpaths are covered with whole processions of laden men and beasts. . . . It may justly be said that it is the fairest time of the year. . . . The Kalends festival banishes all that is connected with toil, and allows men to give themselves up to undisturbed enjoyment.

And here are a few of the "laws" laid down by the Priest of Cronus to cover the Saturnalia.

All business, be it public or private, is forbidden during the feast days, save such as tends to sport and solace and delight. Let none follow their avocations saving cooks and bakers.

All men shall be equal, slave and free, rich and poor, one with another.

Anger, resentment, threats, are contrary to law.

No discourse shall be either composed or delivered, except it be witty and lusty, conducing to mirth and jollity.

The fact that such passages might apply to so many Christmases in the last 1,000 years makes it rather obvious that the

Church Fathers were ultimately successful in regrouping the excitements of the Roman mid-winter about the Mass of Christ, Jesus, becoming the "Unconquered Son" and December 25 emerging as a major feast-day of the Church.

From the fifth to the tenth centuries Christ's Mass marked the start of the ecclesiastical year. By 529 it was a civic holiday, the Emperor Justinian prohibiting work or public business. In 567, the Council of Tours proclaimed the twelve days from December 25 to Epiphany as a sacred, festive season, and established the duty of Advent-fasting in preparation. In 563, the Council of Braga forbade fasting on Christmas Day. Thus a receptacle was being prepared into which all sorts of pagan rites and mid-winter customs could be received as Catholicism moved northwards.

Out on the far reaches of the old Empire, peoples like the Teutons and Celts had their own winter rituals. One of the most important came in mid-November when the pastures were snowed over making it difficult for the cattle to find feed. A great slaughter, feast, and revel was held, summer ended, and the New Year welcomed in. Another was Julmond, ten to twelve days in December when wheat was worshiped, cakes and bread baked, and houses decorated in an effort to gain favor with the field gods. Particular honor was paid to one's ancestors from whom rights to the pastures derived, a thanksgiving still echoed by the Ukrainian custom of referring to a sheaf of wheat as "the forefather."

Such "pagans" lived close to the soil. Their health and survival depended on the fertility of the crops, the animals, and the women. Although there were a number of times in the agricultural year which were crucial, by far the most critical was "after the snows" when the sun weakens, all green has vanished, and man can but hope that "the hound of spring" is truly at "winter's traces." This was the time when sympathetic magic and ritual were called upon to guarantee the return of "light" and growth, when scapegoats were slain or expelled to purge barrenness and evil from the land, when the boar, symbol of regeneration, was sacrificed and consumed. A yule log might be brought in, wished upon, and lighted from the remains of last year's log. A doll, representing the means by which man conquers death, might be placed under the table near the harvest, later to be carried from door to door by women who "carol," hailing the image as both the indicator of feminine power and the rebirth of the sun. Riddles were posed and properly answered, assuring a proper "answer" to the riddle of the season. Liquor was important, for liquor is made from the crops, appears out of ferment as if by magic, has the power to transform, stimulate, and subdue man. Customs of such questionable efficacy as getting cattle drunk or pouring apple-wine on the roots of apple trees to increase yield developed. General inebriation, with resultant gluttony and orgiastic behavior—activities to make the tables and the women groan—were fostered. Sex, death, and rebirth were danced or mimed. Anything that related to fertility, to transformation, to "evergreen" took on significance.

Of course, such conduct wasn't always confined to the mid of winter. Throughout the year, during plowing and seeding, when the first shoots, the first fruits, appeared, the interrelationships of the fertility of crops and animals and women were stressed. Seeds were planted by bouncing them off the buttocks of a wife who had proved a "good breeder"; harvested grain was thrown at the womb of the bride as she wed.

Here and there the conquering Romans joined such ceremonies with their own festivals. However, it wasn't until Christianity came to the tribes that the significant changes were wrought. Then, as had been done with the Saturnalia and the Kalends, the Church Fathers refocused the pagan rites

onto the various holy days, at "summer's end" selecting whatever day was most appropriate to the "first snows" of the region
gaining conversion. As E. K. Chambers wrote in *The Medieval
Stage*, "The winter feast is spread over all the winter half of
the year from All Souls Day to Twelfth night. . . ."—on St.
Martin's Day, November 11; St. Nicholas' Day, December 6;
St. Stephen's Day, December 26; New Year's Day; Old Christmas Day, January 6. And the "parcelling out" was facile: in
the case of December 25, the thanksgiving, the celebration of
regeneration, the presence of the symbolic doll lending themselves to the story of God's "Unconquered Son" quite as if it
had all been written, verily, in the Beginning.

There's little point in trying to summarize centuries of adjustments in custom and calendar as they affect thousands of
persons in dozens of lands. Christianity came to Ireland at the
end of the fifth century; to England, Switzerland, and Austria
during the seventh; to Germany during the eighth; to the
Slavic lands, Hungary, and Scandinavia in the ninth and tenth.
By 1100, for all practical purposes, Europe was converted. Just
about any conceivable combination of pagan and Christian
ritual developed somewhere about Christmas during these
years. Just about any reaction to these combinations developed
somewhere also. The documents of the Middle Ages are fat
with decrees against the abuses of Christmas merriment and
the accompanying desecration of its religious purposes, with
wailings that the Church Fathers are too strict, with indica-
tions that people at large are doing just what they have always
done and paying little attention to the debates of the moral-
ists. Sometimes things were so bad that the Church found it
necessary to associate ritualism with the Devil himself, making
Satan, as it were, the presiding "saint" and labeling the "Saturnalia" involved a communion of witches, Black Mass.

With the Reformation of the sixteenth century, there came

a sharp de-emphasis on Christmas in many lands. After all, Christ-mass, with its major place in the Popish calendar, with its traditional celebration of three Eucharists, with its stress on liturgy and ceremony, was a natural target for many followers of Luther and Calvin. Without going into the casuistry involved, we can realize that while Christ-tide was important to such thinkers, Christ-mass was detestable. In the words of William Prynne, that testy Puritan whose ears were amputated by Charles I,

> Our Christmas lords of Misrule, together with dancing, masques, mummeries, stage-players, and such other Christmas disorders, now in use with Christians, were derived from these Roman Saturnalia and Bacchanalian festivals; which should cause all pious Christians eternally to abominate them.

Yet it has already been stressed that one can't snuff out ritual as though it were a candle, no matter how testy one is. Obviously, many peoples in many lands, even in nations that had become utterly Protestant, went right on with their yule logs, holly, and crèches. But as true religious, and so political, sanction was apt to be lacking, it was not uncommon for the spiritual to give way to the corporal, to nothing but appetite, revel, and debauchery. The result was that in Renaissance Europe three clusters of Christmas celebration bloomed: the medieval, Roman Catholic Christ-mass, which was both spiritual and festive; the Protestant Christ-tide, which was simply spiritual, even severe; and the "neo-pagan" Yuletide, which was quite merry and quite unconcerned with the birth of mankind's Saviour.

Excepting the short rule of Bloody Mary (1553–1558), England was a Protestant nation from 1534 on. As her initial form of Protestantism was neither Lutheran nor Calvinistic, her Christmases tended toward the Yuletide pattern, though

Papists and Puritans snarled in their particular corners. Certainly at courts, where styles were set, the celebration was merry. Henry VIII paid large sums for his mid-winter entertainments, and figures such as £451. 12s. 2d. for "gold stuff" for the "disguysings" or £133. 7s. 5d. for "certen sylks" are not uncommon in his records. Edward Hall, writing in his *Chronicle* of 1542, describes a Christmas celebrated at Greenwich thirty years earlier.

In this yeare the king kept his Christmasse at Greenwich, where was such abundance of viands served to all comers of anie honest behaviour, as hath beene few times seene. And against New Yeeres night was made in the hall a castell, gates, towers, and dungeon, garnished with artillerie and weapon, after the most warlike fashion: and on the front of the castell was written *Le fortresse dangereux,* and, within the castell were six ladies cloathed in russet satin, laid all over with leaves of gold, and everie one knit with laces of blew silke and gold. On their heads, coifs and caps all of gold. After this castell had been caried about the hall, and the queene had beheld it, in came the king with five other, apparelled in coats, the one halfe of russet satin, the other halfe of rich cloth of gold; on their heads caps of russet satin embroidered with works of fine gold bullion.

These six assaulted the castell. The ladies seeing them so lustie and courageous, were content to solace with them, and upon further communication to yeeld the castell, and so they came downe and dansed a long space. And after, the ladies led the knights into the castell, and then the castell suddenlie vanished out of their sights. On the daie of the Epiphanie at night, the king, with eleven other, were disguised, after the manner of Italie; called a maske, a thing not seene before, in England; they were apparelled in garments long and broad, wrought all with gold, with visors and caps of gold. And, after the banket done, these maskers came in, with six gentlemen disguised in silke, bearing staffe torches, and desired the ladies to danse; some were content, and some refused. And, after they had dansed, and commoned together, as the fashion of the maske is, they tooke their leave and departed, and so did the queene and all the ladies.

Henry's daughter by Anne Boleyn enjoyed colorful performances too, some scholars even believing Shakespeare's *Twelfth Night* to have been first staged at Elizabeth's command on January 6, 1601, to honor Don Orsino, Duke of Bracciano. And Ben Jonson's *Christmas His Masque,* done for James I during the year of Shakespeare's death, opens with a parade of "the Sonnes and Daughters" of "Father" Christmas, "being ten in number," led by Cupid "in a string," extravagantly named and "attyred."

MIS-RULE. In a velvet Cap with a Sprig, a short Cloake, great yellow Ruffe like a Reveller, his Torch-bearer bearing a Rope, a Cheese and a Basket.

CAROLL. A Long tawny Coat, with a red Cap, and a Flute at his girdle, his Torch-bearer carrying a Song booke open.

MINC'D-PIE. Like a fine Cookes Wife, drest neat; her Man carrying a Pie, Dish, and Spoones.

GAMBOLL. Like a Tumbler, with a hoope, and Bells; his Torch-bearer arm'd with a Cole-staffe, and a blinding cloth.

POST AND PAIRE. With a paire-Royall of Aces in his Hat; his Garment all done over with Payres, and Purrs; his Squier carrying a Box, Cards, and Counters.

NEW-YEARES-GIFT. In a blew Coat, serving-man like, with an Orange, and a sprig of Rosemarie guilt on his head, his Hat full of Broaches, with a coller of Gingerbread, his Torch-bearer carrying a March-paine, with a bottle of wine on either arme.

MUMMING. In a Masquing pied suite, with a Visor, his Torch-bearer carrying the Boxe, and ringing it.

WASSALL. Like a neat Sempster, and Songster; her Page bearing a browne bowle, drest with Ribbands, and Rosemarie, before her.

OFFERING. In a short gowne, with a Porters staffe in his hand; a Wyth borne before him, and a Bason by his Torch-bearer.

BABIE-CAKE. Drest like a Boy, in a fine long Coat, Biggin, Bib, Muck-
ender, and a little Dagger; his Vsher bearing a great Cake
with a beane, and a Pease.

Others followed suit, William Sandys, writing in his Intro-
duction to *Christmas Carols: Ancient and Modern* notes that:

The noblemen and gentlemen of fortune lived when in the country like petty princes, and in the arrangement of their households
copied that of their sovereigns, having officers of the same name and
import, and even heralds wearing their coat of arms at Christmas, and
other solemn feasts, crying largesse thrice at the proper times. They
feasted in their halls, where many of the Christmas sports were performed. When coals began to be introduced, the hearth was commonly in the middle, whence, according to Aubrey, is the saying,
"Round about our coal-fire." Christmas was considered as the commemoration of a holy festival, to be observed with cheerfulness as
well as devotion. The comforts and personal gratification of their
dependents were provided for by the landlords, their merriment encouraged, and their sports joined. The working man looked forward
to Christmas as the portion of the year which repaid his former toils;
and gratitude for the worldly comforts then received would occasion
him to reflect on the eternal blessings bestowed on mankind by the
event then commemorated.

While Act II of Thomas Middleton's realistic comedy, *The
City Madam*, opens with this exchange concerning city appe-
tites.

SCENE I.—A Room in SIR JOHN FRUGAL's House.

Enter LUKE, HOLDFAST, GOLDWIRE junior, and TRADEWELL junior.

HOLD. The like was never seen.
LUKE. Why in this rage, man?
HOLD. Men may talk of country-christmasses and court-gluttony,

Their thirty-pound buttered eggs, their pies of carps's
  tongues,
Their pheasants drenched with ambergris, the carcases
Of three fat wethers bruised for gravy, to
Make sauce for a single peacock; yet their feasts
Were fasts, compared with the city's.
TRADE. What dear dainty
Was it, thou murmur'st at?
HOLD. Did you not observe it?
There were three sucking pigs served up in a dish,
Ta'en from the sow as soon as farrowèd,
A fortnight fed with dates, and muskadine,
That stood my master in twenty marks apiece,
Besides the puddings in their bellies, made
Of I know not what—I dare swear the cook that dressed it
Was the devil, disguised like a Dutchman.

As the Calvinistic Puritans of the north and midlands began
to make their influence felt in London, all manner of "disguysings" and indulgences (to say nothing of the country revels of the southwest) were bitterly condemned. The purifiers
made a determined effort to abolish Christmas, both as a religious and a popular occasion, arguing that no day should
outrank the Sabbath and that all "unSunday" celebrations were
without dignity. Christmas was forbidden in Scotland as early
as 1583, and by the time of the Commonwealth (1649–1660)
it was made illegal in England. New England was settled in
this atmosphere, and where and while the Puritans dominated,
Christmas was "not merrie" in the brave New World.

Not that the Puritan position was a popular one. In a little
publication of 1653, *The Vindication of Christmas*, Father
Christmas is made to regret the treatment he has received
for the last twelve years. "But," he adds in the traditional opening phrase of the mumming plays, "welcome or not welcome,
I am come!" Both British and Colonial records are laced with

accounts of spectacular and regular breaches of the Puritan wish. And, in spite of pamphlets, sermons, speeches, punishments, incarcerations (town-criers even went their rounds to remind people they must not celebrate Christmas), the feast continued to survive and indeed flourish. Attempted suppression and subsequent rioting became a regular and even welcomed part of the reveling, such phrases as "skull-cracking," "loss of limb," "assault and battery," "fyre and murther" becoming standard phrases in descriptions of the occasion.

Upon Wednesday, Decem. 22, the Cryer of Canterbury by the appointment of Master Major openly proclaimed that Christmas day, and all other Superstitious Festivals should be put downe, and that a Market should be kept upon Christmas day. Which not being observed (but very ill taken by the Country) the towne was thereby unserved with provision, and trading very much hindered; which occasioned great discontent among the people, causing them to rise in a Rebellious way.

The Major being slighted, and his Commands observed only of a few who opened their Shops, to the number of 12 at the most: They were commanded by the multitude to shut up again, but refusing to obey, their ware was thrown up and down, and they, at last, forced to shut in.

The Major and his assistants used their best endeavours to qualifie this tumult, but the fire being once kindled, was not easily quenched. The Sheriffe laying hold of a fellow, was stoutly resisted; which the Major perceiving, took a Cudgell and strook the man; who, being no puny, pulled up his courage, and knockt down the Major, whereby his Cloak was much torne and durty, beside the hurt he received. The Major thereupon made strict Proclamation for keeping the Peace and that every man depart to his own house. The multitude hollowing thereat, in disorderly manner; the Aldermen and Constables caught two or three of the rout, and sent them to Jayle, but they soon broke loose, and jeered Master Alderman.

Soon after, issued forth the Commanders of this Rabble, with an addition of Souldiers, into the high street, and brought with them two Foot-balls, whereby their company increased. Which the Major and Aldermen perceiving, took what prisoners they had got, and would have carried them to the Jayle. But the multitude following after to the King's Bench, were opposed by Captain Bridg, who was straight knoct down, and had his head broke in two places, not being able to withstand the multitude, who, getting betwixt him and the Jayle, rescued their fellowes, and beat the Major and Aldermen into their houses, and then cried Conquest.

Unequivocally, Anglican preachers who had grown up in a Church that had already done its own "purifying" of papistry, resented "latter-day purifiers" who stemmed from Knox and Calvin. Probably as much out of cussedness and political pique as out of religious morality they continued to decorate their churches and hold services on Christmas Day in areas and times when the Puritans were able to tell them not to. John Evelyn describes such a Christmas under Oliver Cromwell.

25th Dec., 1657 I went to London with my wife, to celebrate Christmas-day, Mr Gunning preaching in Exeter chapel, on Micah vii, 2. Sermon ended, as he was giving us the Holy Sacrament, the chapel was surrounded with soldiers, and all the communicants and assembly surprised and kept prisoners by them, some in the house, others carried away. It fell to my share to be confined to a room in the house, where yet I was permitted to dine with the master of it, the Countess of Dorset, Lady Hatton, and some others of quality who invited me. In the afternoon came Colonel Whalley, Goffe, and others, from Whitehall to examine us one by one; some they committed to the Marshal, some to prison. When I came before them, they took my name and abode, examined me why, contrary to the ordinance made, that none should any longer observe the superstitious time of the Nativity (so esteemed by them), I durst offend, and particularly be at Common Prayers, which they told me was but the mass in English, and particularly pray for Charles Stuart; for which we had no scripture. I told them we did not pray for Charles Stuart, but for all Christian Kings, Princes, and Governors. They replied, in so doing we prayed for the King of Spain, too, who was their enemy and a Papist, with other frivolous and ensnaring questions, and much threatening; and, finding no colour to detain me, they dismissed me with much pity of my ignorance. These were men of high flight and above ordinances, and spake spiteful things of our Lord's Nativity. As we went up to receive the Sacrament, the miscreants held their muskets against us, as if they would have shot us at the altar, but yet suffering us to finish the office of Communion, as perhaps not having instructions what to do, in case they found us in that action. So I got home late the next day, blessed be God!

Nonetheless, the Calvinistic tirade, which lasted over a century in Scotland, England, and the New World, had its effect. For some, Christmas became a tide for self-denial. Most, however, were like Miss Mary Lyon, founder and principal of the Mt. Holyoke Seminary, and simply "attended" to the "usual business" of the day. "I have hardly heard a Merry Christmas this morning," she writes in 1847 when Emily Dickinson was there. For such persons, the Christmas celebration simply ceased to be a habit, and December 25 became a church day something less than the modern Easter. In fact, a "bon vers" in Marchmont Needham's 1661 *A Short History of the English Rebellion* says as much,

> *Gone are those golden days of yore,*
> *When Christmas was a high day:*
> *Whose sports we now shall see no more;*
> *'Tis turn'd into Good Friday.*

Thus, it is not hard to believe that no New England college had a "Christmas holiday" in 1847, that December 25 was a common workday in Boston until 1856, that as late as 1870 classes were held in Boston public schools on Christmas, or that one Christmas early in the nineteenth century a master at the Boston Latin School asked the assembled students what day it was and no one knew. For although many of the old ways of celebrating Christmas received free rein with the Restoration and with the dilution of Puritan control in the expanding New England of the late seventeenth and eighteenth centuries, they never again were to be quite the same, and even where feasting, singing, dancing, and decoration were openly enjoyed once more, the indulgence in them was less wholehearted, less enthusiastic.

Soon, "good will toward men" and "alms to the needy" became the melody of "the Christmas carol," a theme quite in harmony with growing skepticisms, growing populations, industrial expansion, and the new *liberté, fraternité, et égalité*. Social concern was elbowing out adoration as the major concern of man, and a new sort of mid-winter rite had arrived, its spirit centered on the fortunes of Tiny Tim and the reformed Scrooge; on the *New York Times* "100 Neediest Families"; on Woody Guthrie's Pretty Boy Floyd who responds to slurs that he's "an outlaw" and "a thief" with the rebuttal. "Well, here's a Christmas dinner for the families on relief."

Much of the emphasis on profound worship that now shows itself in the American Christmas owes its vigor not to the mainstream English stock, but to later immigrants, to the Catholic Irish, Italians, Slavs, Poles, and Latins, to the Lutheran Germans, who have come from areas where the medieval concept of the Christmas holyday was never assaulted as it was in Anglican lands. With their pyramids of candles, their crèches, poinsettias, and *tannenbaums,* they have brought back into the commemoration a wonder that had almost disappeared. As they have shared their ways with their English neighbors, intermarried, and demanded attention, the Christmas of late twentieth-century American has crystallized—an incredible mix of Mass and the masses, miracles and eggnog, camels and reindeer, ecstasy and commercial agony undreamed of in the *auld lang syne.*

2

CHRISTMAS CUSTOMS

W ERE we, like some Squire in some modern Bracebridge Hall, to attempt to observe all the customs and practices
of Christmastide, our fate would be immediate frustration. As
we can guess from the *auld lang syne*, Christmas ways form an
incredible tangle, reaching out from different times, different
cultures, different lands, the roots anchored in Roman festival,
Teutonic worship, Druid idolatry, papistry, protestantism, local
and personal habit, the clusters bound together by the one fact
that they relate *"comme ci, comme ça"* to "the twelve days." In
light of the possibilities, most Americans celebrate quite simply,
contenting themselves with the trimming of a tree, the decoration of the house, a midnight church service for the more determined, and presents, followed by some sort of socializing.
Somewhere, between Christmas Eve and Christmas Night, a
meal, heavy in calories and cholesterol, is served. Few bother
themselves with the wherefores of these activities, most merely
practice them in "the old way" of their parents before them,
making minor adjustments to the whimsies of the marriage
partner, introducing what changes they must stubbornly. Here

and there a household deviates from the bourgeois norm, "because Grandfather always did it that way," "because she is German, you know," "because the kids saw it on television and insist on it." But all in all the twentieth-century American Christmas is far more patterned than one who had just surveyed its yesterdays might suspect—most of the "*auld* acquaintance" scarce remembered, if not totally forgot.

Few Americans, to be sure, bother with a yule log any longer; yet the yule log was once one of the most firmly entrenched of customs. Often a stump or root, it was brought home Christmas Eve, where it was placed in the kitchen hearth or in the main fireplace. It was lighted with a faggot saved from the year before (lest the house burn down) and kept burning for twelve hours (lest ill-luck come). It was not to be bought, but was to be obtained from one's own land or from a neighbor's wood, and it had to ignite the first time (lest trouble follow). In some areas the "log" had to be ash, "the ashen faggot," usually a whole tree, cut up, bound, and drawn to the house by oxen. There it was burned, as people told ghost stories and tales of olden times, drank cider, and watched their shadows on the wall, knowing those without heads would be dead within the year. In Devon, a century ago, thirty-two farms in one postal district still celebrated Christmas Eve by burning "the ashen faggot," but in the city world of today, the faggot and yule log have gone the way of the oxen that drew them home. They have been replaced by the Christmas tree, which became popular as the cities began to grow.

[Lately, a spruce or fir, decked with baubles, bangles, and lights, has been the centerpiece of the celebration. The custom is German, reportedly beginning in the eighth century when St. Boniface dedicated a fir tree to the Holy Child as a counter to the sacred oak of Odin and in the spirit of Tertullian of Carthage, who had stated during a third-century treatise on idolatry,

"You are a light of the world, a tree ever green, if you have renounced the heathen temple, make not such a temple your home." However, the most popular legend insists that the first Christmas tree was cut down by Martin Luther, who brought it home and decorated it with candles to imitate "the starry skies of Bethlehem that Holy Night." Under it, Luther put a crèche and figures of Joseph, Mary, the child Jesus, and various animals.

The first "tree of record" is the one raised in Strassburg in 1604. In 1837, Princess Helen of Mecklenburg brought the custom to France after her marriage to the Duke of Orléans. In 1844, it spread to England when Prince Albert of Saxony and Queen Victoria "had a tree" at Windsor Castle for the pleasure of the royal children. Although Christmas trees were introduced to America with the various waves of German settlement and by the Hessians during the American Revolution, the first national recognition of the custom came in 1856 when Nathaniel Hawthorne's old friend Franklin Pierce decorated one at the White House. By the First World War, community trees at Madison Square Park in New York, on the commons in Boston, on Mt. Wilson in Pasadena were erected, and in the 1920's Altadena developed its famous "Christmas Tree Lane," a mile-long vista of lighted giant deodar cedars. The ninety-foot Norway spruce at Rockefeller Center in 1948 was the tallest tree many people had ever seen, but it was dwarfed by Seattle's 212-footer of 1950. Nevertheless, few trees have symbolized the "ever green" spirit of Tertullian better than the first one known to Clear Creek, Kentucky, cut by Mom Ritchie, folksinger Jean's hill-country mother:

. . . I'd read about 'em having Christmas trees, and I went down the creek way a piece. I'us looking for an evergreen, and I couldn't find one, so I cut a sourwood tree—had all the tags a-hanging on it, and

I decorated it with red ribbon, red paper, popcorn, and red apples.
It pleased the children so well that they've had a Christmas tree
ever since.

Most people have heard that the Christmas tree originates
in the *tannenbaum* and is some sort of vestige of Teutonic
vegetation worship. This is partially true. However, the custom
of using pine and other evergreens ceremonially was well established at the Roman Saturnalia, even earlier in Egypt. St. Boniface didn't choose his fir-tree without precedent. Furthermore,
there had been in the medieval mysteries the dramatic custom
of depicting the entire Garden of Eden by one, apple-decorated
fir, and this did much to tie the evergreen to Christ's birth. The
Paradise play is particularly important. It followed the Expulsion with a hopeful reference to the coming of the Saviour,
and the *paradeisbaum* (the tree of life "in the midst of the garden") was thus linked to the Christmas story. As the Germans
had been accustomed since pagan days to making potted haw-
thorns bloom indoors at mid-winter, they had no difficulty in
welcoming the Christmas *paradeisbaum* to their houses, and the
habit continued after the mysteries were no longer acted. In
addition to apples, the symbols of man's fall, people began to
decorate this "tree of life" with sacramental wafers, the symbols
of man's salvation through the Eucharist. Ultimately, these
symbolisms weakened, and the apples became oranges or
brightly colored balls, the wafers became cookies, often cut like
stars, or angels, animals, and flowers.

A few of the customs associated with the faggot and the yule
log yet linger about the Christmas tree, which in the late
twentieth century is likely to be purchased at the local A&P,
decorated well before Christmas Eve, and disposed of by the
trash collector. Many still feel a powerful compulsion to cut
and bring home their tree, if not from their own land, from "the

neighbor's woods"—which may mean "a front lawn in the suburbs." Some make a family outing of the purchase and decoration. Others refuse to "hang a ball" before Christmas Eve. And a few stolidly burn their withered trees in spite of antipollution ordinances. But as time marches on, artificial trees, television, and the break-up of the family commune may erode such vestiges. The day could come when it will be as unusual to see any tree at all as it is to see your neighbor chop down a local ash, bundle it with withes, and pull it to his hearth by ox-team.

Candles and lights have long been associated with the *tannenbaum*. Perhaps following the lead of the Jews, who celebrate their Hanukkah or Feast of the Lights in December, medieval Church custom identified the candle with Christ, the Light of the World. Candles were placed about the house and in the windows, their smoke seeming to take "flight for heaven" like the frosted prayers of Keats' beadsman, but they didn't begin to appear on the tree itself until the seventeenth century. Before 1600, in Germany, it was customary to ring the tree with candles because the Paradise play was enacted within such a ring, or even to set a pyramid of candles next to the tree. In the Alps, fires are still burned on the mountain slopes on Christmas Eve and each person going to midnight Mass carries a light which sparkles against the pure snow. Many modern Irish families place a candle within a wreath of holly or laurel and burn it through the Holy Night, and in Ireland they will remind you that candles were once lighted in the windows of the "good homes," so that the priest might sneak into the house during Christmas-tide and give Mass unbeknownst to the English. The Catholics would explain the signals by saying, " 'Tis but our hope that Joseph and Mary will be looking for a spot to lie down and will see our candle and choose our home." Mary Vorse describes Portuguese variants of the same customs, explaining in her book *Time and the Town, a Provincetown Chronicle* how *Menin Jesu* used to be celebrated on Cape Cod.

... The older Portuguese people once kept open house from Christmas to New Year's. Every window in their houses had a candle behind it. A home ablaze with lights meant that everyone was welcome, whether or not he knew the host. Indeed, the most welcome and honored guests were the strangers.

In the front room was a pyramid of graduated shelves. One candle on top, on the next shelf two saucers of sprouted wheat; on the next, two candles; on the next, four saucers of sprouted wheat, and so on. These represented the Resurrection and the Light. At the bottom was a crèche of little figures brought from the Western Islands. To everyone who came was given a tiny cordial glass of homemade wine—beach plum, elderberry, or dandelion—and a tiny cake.

This idea of decorating homes on holidays is both worldwide and age-old. It is only natural that in addition to fire and trees, flowers and other plants would be used to "deck the halls" at a ceremony as significant as Christmas. So the Saturnalian laurel, the Teutonic holly, the Celtic mistletoe, and the Mexican poinsettia have all attached themselves to this polyglot ceremony, along with rosemary, ivy, spruce, cherry, lilies, and most anything the land will give forth. Particularly popular in America today is the "flower of the Holy Night," representing the flaming Star of Bethlehem through its red bracts and named after the United States ambassador to Mexico, Joel R. Poinsett. In 1829, he brought the plant back to his home in South Carolina, and its popularity at Christmas has waxed ever since. Mexican legend has the poinsettia originate in a miracle. A poor boy, with nothing to offer Christ at the local church, falls on his knees reassuring God how much he would like to give the gift he has no money to buy. As he rises, there springs from the ground at his feet the first "flower of the Holy Night." He breaks some of the branches with their flaming bracts and lays his gift at the altar.

Many of the plants used at Christmas are symbolic of fertility. Certainly any evergreen (fir, yew, laurel) with its ability to retain verdure in the barren months is appropriate, but by far the most interesting are the holly, the ivy, and the mistletoe. Holly, with its pricking leaves, white flowers, and red berries symbolizes the male reproductive urge. In fact, in the English carols and in the Shrovetide dances, the holly *is* the male and the ivy *is* the female. This use of the plants was most likely borrowed by the Christians along with other customs of the Roman Saturnalia. Later, the Church developed the legend that the Cross was made of hollywood, that the sharp leaves served to form the Crown of Thorns, and that the once yellow berries were stained red by the Lord's blood. The present scrubby appearance of what was once a fine tree can thus be explained as an eternal penance. Nonetheless, holly has its powers, among them an efficacy in curing colic, worms, asthma, smallpox, gout, and dislocated bones. But in Wales it is unlucky to pick holly when the berries are on or to take it into a friend's house where it will cause death. In fact, if one brings it into his own house before Christmas Eve or leaves it there after Twelfth Night, it will cause family quarrels and perhaps bring misfortune for each leaf and each branch. Yet to keep a piece of holly from the church in the house all year is to court good luck, and people in Louisiana still collect the berries after Christmas and hoard them as lucky charms. Like most symbolic plants, holly's story is contradictory and a bit a-logical.

Ivy, holly's mate, also teases one's mind. The plant has long been associated with femininity. In ancient Grecian rites, ivy took its name from the lovely girl who danced with such abandon and joy before Dionysius that she fell dead at his feet. The god, moved by her adoration, turned her into the ivy that she might entwine and embrace whatever is near, indulging, I suppose, her passionate nature. The ivy was traditionally the plant of the Dionysians anyway, in some myths the god's form having developed from it. As Dionysius is the god of wine, ivy is even today the "bush" that "good wine needs not," and reportedly can prevent drunkenness. However, it also has outright fertility properties. In Ireland, collecting ivy leaves and placing them under one's pillow enables one to identify the girl he will marry. And when ivy joins with holly, it takes its place as the un-liberated, subordinate female, the ivy-girl of the holly-boy, and speaks of the willingness of the female to submit. This heritage is what ties the plant to Christianity and Christ-tide. In Church belief, the female ivy is the soul of mankind, submitting to the Lord, and its ever-green symbolizes immortality through the union. Because of its powers, it is widely felt that if an ivy leaf is placed in water in a covered dish during the days from the New Year till Old Christmas it will reveal the future—if spotted predicting sickness and death, if green forespeaking health. But as a medicine, its powers are somewhat limited, working best on minor ailments such as scalds, sunburns, headaches, earaches, and toothaches.

Mistletoe is the most distinguished of all Christmas decorations.

From the centre of the ceiling . . . old Wardle had just suspended, with his own hands, a huge branch of mistletoe, and this same branch of mistletoe instantaneously gave rise to a scene of general and most delightful scrambling and confusion; in the midst of which, Mr. Pickwick with a gallantry that would have done honour to a descendant of Lady Tollimglower herself, took the old lady by the hand, led her beneath the mystic branch, and saluted her in all courtesy and decorum. The old lady submitted to this piece of practical politeness with all the dignity which befitted so important and serious a solemnity, but the younger ladies not being so thoroughly imbued with a superstitious veneration for the custom: or imagining that the value of a salute is very much enhanced if it cost a little trouble to obtain it: screamed and struggled, and ran into corners, and threatened and remonstrated, and did everything but leave the room, until some of the less adventurous gentlemen were on the point of desisting, when they all at once found it useless to resist any longer, and submitted to be kissed with a good grace. Mr. Winkle kissed the young lady with the black eyes, and Mr. Snodgrass kissed Emily, and Mr. Weller, not being particular about the form of being under the mistletoe, kissed Emma and the other female servants, just as he caught them. As to the poor relations, they kissed everybody, not even excepting the plainer portions of the young-lady visitors, who, in their excessive confusion, ran right under the mistletoe as soon as it was hung up, without knowing it! Wardle stood with his back to the fire, surveying the whole scene, with the utmost satisfaction; and the fat boy took the opportunity of appropriating to his own use, and summarily devouring, a particularly fine mince-pie, that had been carefully put by for somebody else.

Now, the screaming had subsided, and faces were in a glow, and curls in a tangle, and Mr. Pickwick, after kissing the old lady as before mentioned, was standing under the mistletoe, looking with a very pleased countenance on all that was passing around him, when the young lady with the black eyes, after a little whispering with the other young ladies, made a sudden dart forward, and, putting her arm round Mr. Pickwick's neck, saluted him affectionately on the left cheek; and before Mr. Pickwick distinctly knew what was the matter, he was surrounded by the whole body, and kissed by every one of them.

Since earliest times in Europe, this hemiparasitic plant, Aeneas' golden bough, has been regarded as mysterious and sacred, symbol of the sun, bestower of life, aphrodisiac, protector against disease and poison. It is widely believed to appear on the host tree, usually the oak, in a flash of lightning. The plant, whose white berries tinge with gold as they wither, was especially sacred to the Celtic Druids. On the sixth night of the moon, a white-robed priest cut the mistletoe with a golden sickle, catching it in a white cloth, never allowing it to touch the ground. Along with two sacrificed white bulls, it was offered in prayer to the gods, symbol of peace and prosperity. Pieces of it were hung above the doors as a signal that old grievances and old enmities were forgot.

As the mistletoe is still ceremoniously plucked by Celtic and Scandinavian peoples at Midsummer Eve, it probably was once particularly associated with that festival, and kissing under it probably didn't become sexual until the custom of kissing among men vanished. On the other hand, Sir James Frazer thought the kissing to be a survival of Saturnalian sexual license. Robert Graves, who is prone to fancy in such matters, suggests that the cutting of the mistletoe from the oak symbolizes the emasculation of the old king (the old year) by the new. The mistletoe, the soul of the oak, must be cut before the tree can be felled and the human proxy of the tree, the old king, slain. Even more spectacular is Britisher R. Reynolds' thesis that mistletoe is considered magic because the plant is propagated by the dung of birds: in the words of Turner's 1532 *Herbal:* "The thrush shiteth out the miscal berries." Dung has long been associated with life-giving properties and fertilization, so the idea isn't that far-fetched. Even the etymology of the word (*mist* means "dung" in German) suggests the theory. At any rate, decorating a house with mistletoe at Christmas is a survival of the New Year's ritual, and whatever the result of these scholarly speculations, English farmers will go right on giving the first cow to calf in the New Year Christmas mistletoe to munch, the plant will continue to be burned on Twelfth Night lest the boys and girls who have embraced beneath it never marry, sprigs of it will be hoarded for burning with next year's yule log or under next year's plum pudding, and there will be excitement when it's hung at Dingley Dell.

Man's eating habits are traditional, too. The "hunting-gathering" primitive gorged himself on meat and more meat after a slaughter, on berries and more berries when the bushes were full, on corn and more corn when the ears ripened. Even after life stabilized around villages and cities, these tendencies persisted, for plenty has a way of appearing suddenly—when the orchards are laden, when the snows fly and the cattle must be killed or left to starve in the uplands, when those ex-urban tomato plants produce five times the crop the Vassar graduate expected. Before the day of canned goods and deep freezers, men had limited choices concerning feasting (or, to be sure, fasting) and the rituals that accompany it.

Even in this industrial age, high up the technological ladder, the eating habits once forced on people by the vagaries of season and agricultural chance have not disappeared utterly. Although modern man might find no occasion to undertake the menu set by Whistlecraft for King Arthur's table—

> ... salmon, venison, and wild boars,
> by hundreds, and by dozens, and by scores.
>
> Hogsheads of honey, kilderkins of mustard,
> Muttons, and fatted beeves, and bacon swine;
> Herons and bitterns, peacocks, swan, and bustard,
> Teal, mallard, pigeons, widgeons, and in fine,
> Plum-puddings, pancakes, apple-pies, and custard.
> And therewithal they drank good Gascon wine,
> With mead, and ale, and cider of our own;
> For porter, punch, and negus were not known.

—he might well indulge in a Thanksgiving or Christmas dinner twice as large as normal, gorge himself at the country club buffet on New Year's Day, or get drunk on purpose New Year's Eve. Even Lent, religious as the fast may now be, still comes at the time of year when fasting was once as much a necessity as an obligation.

Because Yuletide was originally an "end of summer" feast, excesses in food and liquor have always been a centerpiece to its gaiety, its socializing, and its excitement.

> *Yule's come and yule's gane,*
> *And we have feasted weel,*
> *Sae Jock maun to his flail again,*
> *And Jenny to her wheel.*

Moreover, the British people have been particularly identified with indulgence, as witness the Italian metaphor: "busier than an English oven at Christmas." Like many Europeans, they even pamper to the stock at Yuletide, presenting the cattle with a bit of plum pudding and a nip of cider, or, in the Cheshire way, giving "double grain" as St. Francis once insisted "in reverence to the Son of God, whom on such a night the most blessed Virgin did lay down in a stall betwixt ox and ass." As a result, anything like a complete description of British Christmas foods and Christmas beverages is not feasible. Most everything that has been both available and good has graced some table over the years. After all, even a cookie sprinkled with red and green sugar will qualify as a Christmas delicacy. Yet "holiday staples" have developed. For instance, today's Americans keep the turkey farms in business by insisting on "a bird" for both November and December. Of course, the American turkey is a recent entrée, its vogue not beginning till the seventeenth century. The boar's head has been far longer celebrated by time, pomp, and circumstance.

Devout Christians will imply that the boar's head was introduced to the Christ-mass feast to indicate abhorrence of Judaism. But the swine was a sacrificial animal for the Teutonic Yule perhaps because it commonly destroyed crops, though most likely because of its connection with Frey and Freya and with that abundant boar of Northern mythology, Schrimnir, whose ever-renewing flesh feeds the heroes of Valhalla. Be that as it may, the ushering in of the boar's head early established itself in the English Christmas and remained a widespread custom on estates, at court, and in the colleges till the end of the thirteenth century when wild boars began to become extinct in the Isles. Here and there "bringing in the boar" endured longer, and at places like Queen's College, Oxford, became an honored tradition. Sandys quotes a description of one such entrée, from the "Christmas Prince":

At the time of the celebrated Christmas Prince, at St. John's, Oxford, in 1607, "The first messe was a boar's head, wch was carried by ye tallest and lustiest of all ye guard, before whom (as attendants) wente first, one attired in a horseman's coate, wth a boar's speare in his hande, next to him an other huntsmañ in greene, wth a bloody faucion drawne; next to him 2 pages in tafatye sarcenet, each of y^{em} wth a messe of mustard; next to whome came hee y^t carried ye boares-head crost wth a greene silke scarfe, by wch hunge ye empty scabbard of ye faulcion, wch was carried before him. As y^{ei} entred ye hall, he sange this Christmas Caroll, ye three last verses of euerie staffe being repeated after him by ye whole companye."

Boar's head has now disappeared as an item on the Christmas menu. That it's place would be assumed in "these giddy-paced times" by foods easier to prepare is clarified by a quick perusal of the following directions for "a simple way" of preparing the dish. The recipe assumes you have found, slain, and beheaded a wild boar to start with.

Split the head in two halves, except for the joining skin at the top. Remove the eyes, ears, snout, and all the bone at the back. Wrap the brains separately. Soak all parts in running water for an hour,

rub with salt, and leave to soak in a tub of strong saltwater overnight.

The next day, drain, wipe dry, and rub well with pickling spice,
black pepper, salt and saltpetre (one dram of the former to one
ounce of the latter), then lay in a large earthenware basin, which
it will soon fill with brine. Turn and rub with salt and the brine
daily for a week.

At the end of a week or ten days, drain. You now have a piece of
salt pork which can be plain boiled or baked. However, it is best
put to boil very gently with vegetables: large amounts of sage,
onion skins, bay, peppercorns, and marjoram. The piece should
simmer until all the bones are loose. Allow it to cool in the broth,
then remove the bones carefully. The tongue should be skinned
and replaced, and the hot meat trussed into a conical shape. Dust
it with powdered mace and pepper, tie it firmly into shape, and
leave it overnight under some sort of weight.

The ears, bone, gristle, and other odd parts should continue to be
boiled with additional herbs and spices until stiff. Add a tablespoon-
ful of brown vinegar and a couple of crushed eggshells (to give
clearness) and strain the glaze into a jar. By the time the boar's head
is cold, the glaze should have solidified into a stiff brown jelly.
Brush the jelly over the cold head, glazing it till smoothly coated.
The final coating should be poured on and left to set.

Serve on a clean flat fir bough on a carving board, adding split
almond tusks, with prunes for eyes. Trim with parsley, lemon peel,
vegetables, and a holly wreath. Place a bowl of hot mustard sauce
alongside.

"This," as one cook notes, "is a very savory form of cold bacon."
But one does see why it has given way here to pickled swine's
flesh (brawn), there to roast beef, capon, goose, and American
turkey.

But other meats and the fowls were often elaborately prepared, too—frequently in pies. The most famous pie in the
annals of Christmas was one served at Sir Henry Grey's in
London in 1770. It was nine feet in circumference, weighed
twelve stone, and was pushed into the dining hall on wheels. In

it were four geese, four wild ducks, two woodcocks, two "turkies," four partridges, seven blackbirds, six pigeons, two rabbits, two neat's tongues, two bushels of flour, twenty pounds of butter, and sundry items. It is small wonder that there is a southwestern English saying: "The Devil himself dare not appear in Cornwall during Christmas for fear of being baked in a pie."

The Puritans thought he had been baked into mince pie, the contents of which are meant to symbolize the variety of gifts offered by the Magi at the *crèche*. Developed from the various meat and fowl pies with the knowledge of spices gained during the Crusades, mince pies should be made in the oblong shape of a manger with an image of the baby Jesus on top. It was this reproduction of the Christ that aroused Puritan ire, and one labeled himself Anglican (or even worse, Roman Catholic) by serving such an abomination during the seventeenth and eighteenth centuries. Mince pies were actually illegal during the Commonwealth and during the earlier years in New England where the custom was transferred without the Christ image to Thanksgiving. It was during these years that the oblong shape began to disappear also. An Anglican, baking her family's "Christmas pie" in circular shape and decorating it with evergreens, could "disguise" its inner nature. After the Restoration, the refusal of Presbyterians to eat mince pie was a stubborn point of honor—a matter well illustrated by John Bunyan's scorn when one was offered him in prison.

Pies and cakes using vegetables have also been a traditional part of the Christmas feast. Originally, the flour used in these delicacies had mystic significance, and in many places they were tasted by each person who entered the home on Christmas Day. Some families baked a cake for each member of the household, and considered those whose cakes cracked marked for ill-luck or death. In the poem "Twelfe Night" Robert Herrick de-

scribes the custom of the "King's Cake," made containing a
bean or a hard kernel of corn and served on Epiphany Day.
The person getting the bean or kernel is named king, in a selec-
tion most reminiscent of pagan ways of selecting a ruler for the
New Year.

> *Now, now the mirth comes*
> *With the cake full of plums,*
> *Where Beane's the King of the sport here;*
> *Beside we must know,*
> *The Pea also*
> *Must revell, as Queene, in the Court here.*
>
> *Begin then to chuse,*
> *(This night as ye use)*
> *Who shall for the present delight here,*
> *Be a King by the lot,*
> *And who shall not*
> *Be Twelfe-day Queene for the night here.*

"Frumenty" or "furmety" (it's name derives from the Latin
word for corn) is also made of hulled wheat, boiled in milk and
seasoned with cinnamon, sugar, and various spices. It may have
originated in cereal sacrament too. In Staffordshire and Yorkshire, the wheat to be used was customarily hung in a sheaf in
the kitchen and the dish was the first thing consumed Christmas
morning. In similar fashion, the Scots ate their sowens (a thick
syrup) in bed before rising Christmas Day. Such fruit and grain
dishes, as well as pies and cakes shaped like animals, are surely
vestiges of and replacements for what was once ritualistic eating
and animal sacrifice. Related customs are far more elaborate
on the continent, where in Sweden and Denmark "Yule Boars,"
loaves in the form of pigs, are still placed on the tables during
the Christmas season or where in Germany plum-loaf biscuits
called *stollen* are baked in animal and human forms. Plum

pudding or "hackin," made of hacked fruits and vegetables
drenched with liquor and decked with holly still carries this
sort of symbolism to the modern table. Plum pudding, if prepared traditionally, should be made during the first week of
Advent and everyone in the household, even the infant-in-arms,
has to help stir the ingredients.

But food claims small precedent over drink. Whether it is the
beer, ale, and sweet wines of the feudal feast, the "Christmas
whiskey" of the frontier Baptist, or the eggnog of Pleasant
Valley, U.S.A.; whether the "geese-dancers" take a nip in the
orchard, whether Goody brings forth the "nut-browne ale" as
the games are called, whether the bar-keep sets up "freebies"
for the backroom boys, Christmas spirits have been, surely will
be, and are synonymous with the Christmas spirit.

> Wisselton, wasselton, who lives here?
> We've come to taste your Christmas beer.
> Up the kitchen and down the hall,
> Holly, ivy, and mistletoe;
> A peck of apples will serve us all,
> Give us some apples and let us go.
>
> Up with your stocking, on with your shoe,
> If you haven't any apples, money will do.
> My carol's done, and I must be gone,
> No longer can I stay here.
> God bless you all, great and small,
> And send you a happy new year.

The most elaborate form of Christmas imbibition takes its
name from the Anglo-Saxon term "waes hael" (be whole or
hale). Today, true Christmas wassailing has pretty well vanished,
and in America vestiges of this tradition of going from house to
house, caroling, being fed, and socializing are more vigorous
at Hallowe'en than they are at Christmas. Wassailing was origi-

nally an important part of agricultural ritual: in England, at least, focused on the apple orchards. The idea was to salute the trees in the dead of winter to insure a crop for the coming year. The brew used was usually mulled cider or ale with roasted apples and perhaps egg in it. The date varied across the twelve days, from Christmas Eve to Epiphany, with Old Christmas morning the most popular. If done formally, the wassail procession visited the principal orchards of the parish, caroling and even mumming as it went. In each orchard, major trees were selected and the roots were sprinkled with the liquor or a bowl of the liquor was broken against the trunk like champagne on a ship. Incantations such as,

> Stand fast at root,
> Bear well at top,
> Every twig bear apple big,
> Every bow bear apple now

or,

> Here's to thee old apple tree,
> Hats full, sacks full,
> Great bushel bags full,
> Hurrah!

were quoted and great noise, terrorizing evil spirits, was made by firing a gun, by blowing on a bullhorn, or by shouting. Before proceeding, the procession usually danced about the honored tree or snaked its way out of the orchard. That summer and fall the care with which the ceremony had been executed was measured by the size and health of the yield.

Some tags of all this remain in practices like the incessant cocktail parties of the modern bourgeois Christmas or the out-

land drinking customs recorded by Herbert Halpert in Deep
Harbour, Newfoundland.

The mood of Christmas is set to a great extent by the groups of
social drinkers who spread the spirit from house to house. On an
evening when there are many groups of men "on the go" the entire
community is influenced by the air of excitement and anticipation
created by their singing. Throughout the earlier part of the evening
and into the early hours of morning, others join existing groups
and new groups are formed.

In most cases the groups start out after supper; they leave their
houses between 7:00 and 8:00 P.M. and continue with their celebrations until three or four the next morning. Carousing around for
eight or more hours whets the appetite, and towards the end of their
house visits, one of the men might suggest to those in his group
that everyone come over to his house for a "scoff." This late supper
might include a meal of "bottled moose meat," warmed-over soup
from the Church of England Women's Association "time," homemade sweet bread, "pork-buns," and "a good cup of tea."

There are several patterns of visiting followed by both mummers
and social-drinking men. First, men stop in succession at the houses
of each man in the group. In this way everyone becomes a host in
turn, reciprocating the hospitality he has received. If the "crowd"
has not had time to stop at each of the houses, the same men may
start off together the next night.

Another pattern followed by both groups is that the men will
stop at the houses of those who have earlier visited them. One man
might say, "Let's go over to Bill's now, he told me to come over."
Bill's invitation was not for a specific night; he was fulfilling his
side of an obligation when he extended the invitation. The men
may go to a house because they expect "a good drink of rum," or because the host is known for his particularly fine homebrewed beer.
The sounds of singing men, accordion music, and step-dancing may
also draw a group into a house.

There are, however, some houses at which no one will stop; these
houses do not provide any drinks because the owners do not drink.
One of these men has said, "The only reason men come to visit
during Christmas is to get a drink. They don't come to see *you*."

The custom of carrying a "wassail cup" or "wassail bob" from door to door, and probably the custom of the quite stationary punch bowl, both derive from this "saluting of the orchards" as it fused with the practice of reproducing the crèche in the churches. In the north of Britain a little "wassail bob" or vessel is carried about by singing villagers. The bob contains two wax figures lying amid decorations of ribbons, fruit, evergreens, and flowers, one representing the Virgin Mother, the other the Infant Christ. The local name for the bob is "the-doll-in-the-box." Rhymes called "vessel" or "wassail" songs, developing themes like,

> *Wassail, wassail, 'round the town,*
> *Our bread is white, our ale is brown.*

or,

> *God bless the master*
> *And his lady too,*
> *And all the little children*
> *That round the table go*

are commonly heard where the "doll-in-the-box" exists, but longer pieces like the "Holy Well" carol or city ballads such as "The Bailiff's Daughter of Islington" serve too.

More recently the "doll-in-the-box" has given away to the "Christmas Box" which is taken around on either December 25 or on St. Stephen's, the twenty-sixth, a day widely called "Boxing Day." The Christmas Box may have started as a church charity. Boxes were customarily placed in the churches for contributions after the Christmas Day services, and on the twenty-sixth the money so gathered was distributed by the priests to the poor. The idea was taken over by apprentices and tradesmen's assistants who carried a box to the homes of their masters' customers asking for gratuities. Soon scavengers pretending to be "in the trades" carried phony boxes around. Then children took up the practice, almost on a Hallowe'en basis, though the threat they used was apt to be "ill-luck or treat" rather than "trick or treat." In spite of what some claim, the custom has never been connected to the habit of dedicating a box to a patron saint before a sea-voyage, then putting money in it after each shipboard Mass—the money to be collected later by the local priest and purportedly spent to encourage forgiveness for whatever debaucheries had occurred while the sailors were beyond parish surveillance. Such "boxing" is not specifically connected to "the twelve days."

True boxing, a relatively recent form of Christmas giving, is of course a gratuity for the poor, a charity. There is no exchange of presents. The Romans gave each other gifts—food, candles, trinkets, or statues of appropriate gods—during the mid-winter Kalends, and offered material thanks to the Emperor as well. The custom was called *Strenae* and is still practiced in France where *étrenne* are interchanged in January. It is pretty obvious that the *Strenae* custom was transferred by the Christians to December 25, where it eventually absorbed the other giving practices associated with St. Martin (November 11) and St. Nicholas (December 6), saints who rewarded good children and switched the bad. Christmas giving was also encouraged by the belief that the shepherds, Wise Men, and others presented their King with gifts in his manger. In addition, gift-giving is connected to church and house decorations. Originally, the Romans exchanged twigs from the sacred grove of the goddess Strenia at mid-winter, associating them with good will and happiness for the coming year and hanging them about the house for luck. It is even possible that the bundle of faggots carried by St. Martin, St. Nicholas, and their predecessors, although used to whip bad children, originated in the lucky branches of Rome.

In one form or other, we still practice these ways of exchanging gifts. Besides the stocking left full by a Santa who has come to town and determined which child was "nice" and not so "naughty" after all, we have the "his" and "hers" presentations of power tools and fur coats, similar to, if more elaborate than, the twigs and trinkets of *Strenae*. Also like the Romans, we offer the "emperor" a fifth of Canadian whiskey, not just in exchange for the transistor radio he mass orders for the entire office staff but also to make sure "the old boy is well oiled for the coming year." Our ancestors knew all about this sort of thing, too. In 1561–1562, Good Queen Bess received presents like "£40 in a red silk purse" and a great number of articles of dress, "most of them richly wrought," from constituents like Matthew Parker, Archbishop of Canterbury, and John Betts, "servaunte of the Pastrye." In return, she gave presents of plate gilt all around. And her half-sister Mary got everything from "the fore part of a kyrtell, and a peire of sleves of cloth of silv', richly enbraudered all ouer with Venice silver" to "a fatte goose and a capon" in exchange for her bloody benevolences.

The Christmas card is, of course, a cheap present, like the Roman trinket including a happy wish for the New Year. The practice of sending them is relatively recent and probably began with the English "schoolpieces" or "Christmas pieces" which were simple pen and ink designs on sheets of writing paper. The first formal card was supposedly designed by an Englishman, J. C. Horsley, in 1843. It was lithographed on stiff, dark cardboard and depicted, in colors, a party of grown-ups and children with glasses of wine raised in a toast over the words "A Merry Christmas and a Happy New Year to you." One thousand were printed, and one sent to James Peters, his wife and family, from John Washbourn and his wife of 22 Theberton Street in Islington, London, still survives. Now over a billion cards are sold each year in Britain and the United States alone.

"Get together" activities like wassailing, boxing, and gift-giving encourage playing as well as drinking, and many sorts of games have had their Christmas day. In our time the entertainment may be an NFL play-off or three periods of hockey on color TV; yesteryear it was musical chairs, "hunt the slipper," cards, forfeits, riddling, or "blindman's buff." Perhaps "blindman's buff" is the most traditional of them all. Widely known by names derived from animals, like "blind cow" or "blind mouse," it was originally played with masks and probably descends directly from ceremonies involving the animal sacrifices of the winter solstice. Riddling has a similar origin. An "enigma" like

> Flower of England, fruit of Spain,
> Met together in a shower of rain,
> Put in a bag and tied with a string.
> If you guess the answer, I'll give you a pin.

—with its solution: either a man and a woman married or a Christmas pudding—may well retain faded vestiges of agricultural ritual. Success or failure in answering riddles such as this was once associated with success or failure in planting, breeding, health, and war. Riddles properly answered also indicated one's affiliation with special groups like the priests, the warriors, the women who have passed through puberty. Many are obscene and, in order to deceive evil spirits, sacrilegious: "Who was the sexiest man in history? Christ, because he rose after he was dead," or "Here's to the dark lane and the red entry, where one goes in and two stand sentry." Riddling sessions invariably ran the danger of becoming "dirty joke sessions" as the bowl went round and the toasts roared forth. In fact, much Christmas game-playing, awash as it was in cider, ale, and whiskey, was followed by some sort of license: dancing, kissing, and that play best suited to the beef-fed farmer and his ruddy hoyden or to the rake and his tender Chlöe.

Perhaps the most spectacular account of a Christmas game is the one of a football match observed by antiquarian Laurence Gomme in South Cardiganshire, Wales, about 1887. This annual contest, participated in by the entire community (regardless of sex, age, or status), was little more than a huge fight between peoples who felt their ancestry to be pure-bred Irish and those who felt theirs to be pure-bred Brython. After the morning service on Christmas Day, the opposing "teams" assembled on the turnpike between the highlands and the lowlands. A ball was thrown into the air and from then on play was, you could say, "sudden death." The "Irish" could score and so win by getting the ball up the mountainside to their village of Rhyddlan at the top, while the "Brythons" prevailed if they got the ball to their town of New Court at the lower end of the parish. Few holds were barred, and hook, as well as crook, prevailed. The custom is clearly a survival from the earliest of times when, as has been shown in the case of Roman soccer or American Indian lacrosse, woolly sports contests replaced outright war in settling rivalries between villages, clans, and even tribes.

A somewhat different, if no less violent, kind of "game" was the hunting of the wren, a Christmastide custom usually reserved for St. Stephen's Day. A wren was sought out, killed, spitted on a pole or placed on a bed of evergreen or furze, and carried about the community by the "hunters" who asked for gifts and, like wassailers, sang songs such as:

> The wren, the wren, the king of birds,
> St. Stephen's Day, was killed in the furze.
> Although he is little his honor is great,
> And so good people, pray give us a treat.

or,

> *We hunted the wren for Robin the Bobbin,*
> *We hunted the wren for Jack of the Can,*
> *We hunted the wren for Robin the Bobbin,*
> *We hunted the wren for everyone.*

Those who did contribute usually got a feather from the bird in exchange.

The wren is popularly called "the king of the birds" and on ordinary days it would be unlucky to kill one. Thus the Christmas hunt may be a survival of the winter custom of slaying a divine animal, symbol of the king of the old year, and may well have become associated with the birth and rebirth of Christ in some places. Certainly, as the wren is carried from home to home and its feathers are shared by benevolent residents, the supposed powers of the little bird are distributed to men of good will.

Squirrels, foxes, cats, and owls sometimes met the same ceremonial death. Hunting the squirrel is an especially difficult "game." As the animal races about the trees, leaping from limb to limb, the men and boys try to hit him with a willowy stick about fifteen inches long with a pear-shaped ball or lump of lead at the tip. The weapon, named a "squail" or a "snogg," depending on its construction, is hurled at the squirrel with amazing skill, sometimes from a hundred fifty feet away. The dead squirrels are boiled and eaten.

Behind all these mid-winter activities lies a welter of isolated superstitions and beliefs which groups here and there trust or feel they should observe. Many people still half-believe (in Hardy's words "hoping it might be so") that the cattle will kneel down as the Holy Midnight comes, or that the bees will hum the *100th Psalm* on Christmas Eve. Others feel that a ghost can't walk on the Holy Night. Marcellus in *Hamlet,* referring to the apparition of Hamlet's father, says.

> *It faded on the crowing of the cock.*
> *Some say that ever 'gainst that season comes*
> *Wherein our Saviour's birth is celebrated,*
> *This bird of dawning singeth all night long,*
> *And then, they say, no spirit dare walk abroad,*
> *The nights are wholesome, then no planets strike,*
> *No fairy takes, nor witch hath power to charm.*
> *So hallowed and so gracious is that time.*

The list is almost without end: a windy Christmas is a sign of good fortune; a cricket chirping at Christmas brings good luck; a person born on Christmas Day can see revenants; if one opens the doors as the clock strikes midnight on Christmas Eve the house will be rid of all evil spirits; there will be a death in the family before the New Year is out if you have used yew in the house decorations; you will have one lucky month for each cook whose pudding you eat Christmas Day; if fire is carried from the house on Christmas Day it will bring trouble; and so on. Many of the superstitions involve timing, telling how unlucky it is to light the yule log before Christmas Eve, to burn the house decorations on any day but Candlemas, or to take the tree down after Old Christmas. Others center on the misfortune that is associated with animals or plants who participated in the Crucifixion or offended the Holy Family in some fashion: the ass who belched at the crèche, the rush used to switch the child Jesus, the holly whose prickles made the Crown. Some are weather beliefs, offering such agricultural wisdom as this: if the sun shines through the fruit trees at noon on Christmas the crop will be full; if it is partly cloudy at noon the crop will be half-full; if it is cloudy or rainy, there will be no harvest at all. Often, such predictions are conveniently packaged in small poems:

If Christmas on a Sunday (Thursday) be,
A windy winter we shall see.

Hours of sun Christmas Day,
So many frosts month of May.

Christmas bells on Saturday tolled,
Winter foggy, summer cold.

It has long been thought that bells and chimes must be sounded Christmas Day, probably not so much to express joy as to frighten evil spirits. Hand-bell ringers accompany wassailers and carolers, as do youngsters whose job it is to fire guns and raise a general commotion. This faith in noise has spawned the belief that church bells destroyed or broken on Christmas Day will nonetheless ring every December 25 from then on. There is even a legend in Nottinghamshire of a Christmas earthquake that buried a church, bells and all, deep in the ground. Still, the catastrophe was powerless to prevent the chimes from being heard every Christmas thereafter.

Superstitions about "first footing" or "letting in Christmas" center on the first human to enter a house on Christmas Day. Known as "the lucky bird," the person's sex and hair-color are crucial. Where this custom is prevalent, it is generally believed that no one should leave the house on Christmas morning until "the lucky bird" has entered. For good luck, the first footer should be a dark-haired man, and he must not be turned away. Usually he carries a sprig of evergreen and will enter at the front door, proceed through the house, and leave by the rear. En route, he may be given a gift of salt, bread, pins, money, or some trinket. In many towns, he is a professional hired specifically to "let in Christmas." But professional or amateur, he must not have red hair. Although red hair was considered sinister long before Christ, Christians associate the color with Judas Iscariot. In some places, groups of first footers make the rounds, much like wassailers, boxers, and wren-hunters, singing songs as they move from home to home.

> I wish you a merry Christmas
> And a happy New Year;
> A pocket full of money
> And a cellar full of beer,
> And a great fat pig
> To last you all the year.

To allow a woman to "let in" Christmas is to court disaster. There was a time in Herefordshire (and I am sure in other areas) when no woman was allowed in the house all Christmas Day long.

Nevertheless, for the young lady who wishes to improve her love life, few times of the year serve her better than Christmastide. Her packaged opportunities run the gamut, from sleeping on a piece of Christmas cake to dropping a bit of her menstrual fluid into the favored man's Christmas beer. The trick that serves as a backdrop to Keats' *Eve of St. Agnes* is as efficacious during the twelve days as it is the night of January 20. The girl is to place her shoes on either side of her bed, put rosemary in one and thyme in the other; then, sleeping on her back, she shall dream of the man she is to marry. The single girl may also approach the door of the henhouse on Christmas Eve, tap it smartly, and wait. If a hen cackles first, the chances for marriage during the coming year are poor. If a cock crows, the future is bright. She can join her sisters in naming the bands that bind the "ashen faggot." The girl who has given her name to the first band to burn through will be

the first wed. She can put lead in a cup of water at midnight
Christmas Eve. The shape it takes will indicate the profession
of her husband: nails for a carpenter, horse-shoes for a black-
smith, etc. A coffin-shape means her bridegroom is to be death.
She can make a dough-cake in silence, place it on the hearth,
and still in silence prick her initials on the surface. At midnight Christmas Eve, if she watches, she will see her future
husband enter the room, go to the hearth, and prick his initials beside hers. Christmas morning, she can walk backwards
toward a pear tree, circle it three times, then look up to see
the image of her future husband appear among the branches.
She can conjure the same image by picking twelve sage leaves
in the garden at midnight Christmas Eve. But perhaps most
sentimental of all, she can keep the rose which she plucked on
Midsummer's Day. It will still be fresh Christmas morning,
and if she wears it to church, her future husband will come
to take it from her.

One mid-winter morning just before the First World War,
heiress, folklorist, Elsie Clews Parsons took notes as she sat in
a shabby farmhouse in Guilford County, North Carolina:

"Nex' Friday will be Ol' Christmas," said Henry Stockton, a Negro
of about forty, before whose fireplace I was at the time sitting. "My
gran'mammy used to take a piece of coal an' mark up here each
day after Christmas for twelve days" and he pointed to the white-
washed lintel of the fireplace.

By him and by many others, old and young, white and colored,
I was told that on Old Christmas "day broke twice," that the Poke
stalks and the hop-vines put up early in the morning to go back
again when the sun is well up; and that before "sun-up," or more
commonly at midnight, the beasts, the cows, and the horses fell on

their knees to pray. "We had an ol' horse called Nellie," said one girl, "an' one year Popper took us out to see her at midnight. She was sure lyin' down."—"I'd like to go out to the barn to see," said an older white woman.

On Old Christmas even to-day the older people will not work. One old colored woman had a story of how one year in her youth her mother had forgotten about the day, and was spinning. Her mother's sister came in, and exclaimed about it. "But it's not Ol' Christmas," said her mother. "Yes, 'tis. I know it is Ol' Christmas, because I saw the hop-vines up." Apart from not working on the day, there seems to be no other way of celebrating.

I may add that formerly in celebrating Christmas, old people told me, the stocking of a naughty child would be filled with switches, and switches only. Aunt Lamy Tatum told me that her mother's threat of these switches made her good before Christmas. Aunt Lamy's great-nephew believed in the filler of stockings, in Santa Claus, until he was eighteen.

Elsie Parsons' description summarizes vividly the confusion of custom, belief, migration, and cross-cultural influence that floats in the wake of anyone's Christmas—the residue of man's relentless attempt to explain life and order his thoughts. And if the evolution of that tangle is as complex and baffling to search as that of sea weeds churned up in the wake of some actual ship, we must also recall that this welter of practices is not the possession of the ignorant and the benighted alone. For even the highly schooled mind, which may question the Christian explanation itself, can feel uncomfortable if forced to break Christmas custom or overlook Christmas superstition. It is not only the country farmer who harbors a bit of the yule log to toss on the blaze of next year or who busses beneath the mistletoe. Such things are the habit of lawyers, Wall Street wizards, and leftist professors whose minds brook little traffic with illogic, magic, and the like.

3

THE STARDUST OF A MEMORY

THE date of Jesus' birth was set at the year 1 in the
mid-sixth century when Dionysius Exiguus arranged the Christian calendar. Reckoning as best he could, he figured Christ to
have been born 754 years after the founding of Rome, when
Herod the Great (appointee of the Roman Senate) was ruler of
Judea. Just after Jesus' birth, Herod issued that most famous
order demanding the elimination of all boys in Bethlehem
under two. Although modern scholarship has established that
only fifteen to thirty of the town's 2,000 residents could possibly
have been slain, the event has been symbolically labeled the
"Slaughter of the Innocents" and Christian fancy has "piled the
bodies high." Certainly, the order must have been routine for
a king who is given credit for engineering the deaths of his
mother-in-law, his brother-in-law, his uncle, his wife, and a
legion of conspirators and antagonists. At any rate, Herod
seems to have died about April 1, 4 B.C., and if this is so,
Dionysius has to be at least four years off in dating Christ's birth.

Mary probably labored in one of the limestone caves used to
shelter animals near Bethlehem, and the crib was hollowed out

47

of the limestone wall and lined with clay. A specific cave, which
was reported locally as the place of the Saviour's birth during the
centuries after the event, was desecrated by the Romans. Later
they made it into a grotto to honor Adonis, Aphrodite's lover,
who met death at the tusks of a boar. It wasn't until 325 that
the converted Constantine ordered a great church built there.
Buffeted, spared, and repaired throughout a series of rebellions
and invasions, this church has served as a goal of Christian
pilgrims for hundreds and hundreds of years. Today it is called
"St. Mary of the Nativity" and the grotto has walls and flooring
of decorated white marble. The spot where Christ is believed
to have been born is marked by a silver star and the Latin in-
scription: *Hic de Maria Virgine, Jesus Christus natus est.*

Jesus, "the Anointed," died in a year usually called 33 A.D.,
crucified by the Jewish Sanhedrin, the National Council, because His claims to being The Messiah were deemed seditious.
It was a fate that has not been uncommon to radical leaders.
Most of what we know about His parents and the events of His
short life come to us from documents and gospels recorded
no sooner than 25 and very probably much nearer 75–125 years
after His Crucifixion. The result is that we rely heavily on oral
tradition for nearly all we know about Christ. It is sensible to
believe that this oral tradition, whether transmitted by the folk
or by more sophisticated and scholarly churchmen, is subject
to the same laws that oral tradition is ever subject to.

As a theologian speaking of Jesus, C. S. Lewis was able to pro-
claim that "Either this man was, and is, the Son of God: or else
a madman or something worse." But such a statement is scarcely
satisfactory to the folklorist. Folklorists, by their training, are
compelled to see Jesus in terms of other mythologies, other
bodies of legend, other cultures that have existed across the
world. Long ago, they might have disclaimed His historicity,
marking the entire story as but a variant of the pagan sun-god

myths, with birth at the winter solstice and regeneration at the vernal equinox—a position still popular with the "radical critics" of religious studies. But the modern folklorist is both more conservative and more sophisticated. He accepts the historical Christ, though he sees Him (almost as a Jew or Unitarian might see Him) not as divine, but as a human being whose life was deemed heroic, the story first becoming legendary, eventually to be encrusted with mythological and miraculous motifs. In fact, the story as we know it follows the very pattern that the trained folklorist would predict: mixing biographical fact with anecdotes once ascribed to earlier prophets or ingeniously composed by some Near Eastern Parson Weems. The best known of these Jesus legends entered the Bible, where, selected under the influence of Divine inspiration, they became myths: the rest remained a part of church literature and oral tradition, where from time to time they have cropped out in apochryphal writings, hagiographa, ballads, folktales, and anecdotes.

So the folklorist sees exceptional beauty, but little else unusual, in the narratives that concern Christianity's Saviour. Christ's birth to a virginal mother, the seminal flow of the Father passing into her immaculate body like sunshine through the rosy window of a medieval cathedral, simply echoes the conception narratives of other heroes in other lores of other lands, as do such details as the Wise Men and the Eastern Star, the amazed shepherds, the host of heralding angels, the varied visions of the heavenly creatures. The story of the desperate King Herod attempting to kill the infant Saviour is a stock first act in the drama of many heroic lives; the betrayal by the trusted Judas, a stock dénouement. Nor is there much new in the epilogue that He, the incarnation of his follower's ideals, did not really die after His Crucifixion, but has gone to a heaven to await that Day when He can once again serve His people. Other heroes in other mythologies, figures like Oedipus, Theseus, Hercules, Perseus, Jason, Dionysius, Apollo, Moses, Raven, and Coyote have their unusual conceptions in showers of gold, beneath the embrace of lusting swans, through cedar leaves swallowed in drinking water; are tested in the crib by serpent and sword; are hidden among the bullrushes; live out their model lives till betrayed by treachery or thunderclap; and are carried off to some Avalon beyond some Asgard to await the recall of the worshipers.

Folklorists feel contented when arranging the synoptic gospels in the order of their composition, noting that Mark, the earliest, has no infancy narratives and no mention of the Virgin birth, while such stories do appear in Luke, Matthew, and especially John which were written three to perhaps five generations after Christ died. They also note that the portions of Mark (xvi, 9–20) in which Jesus miraculously appears to Mary Magdalene and others after His death and which were included into the King James and the Rheims-Douai bibles is clearly the work of some editor who lived in the second century.

The accretion of such materials and the constant expansion of the Christian biography continues if one pursues the matter into the later apochrypha, hagiographic transcriptions, and writings of the Church Fathers. As the generations pass, Jesus' life and activities, along with those of Mary and Joseph, become less historical, more and more miraculous; less legendary, more mythological. In the Eastern Church, the Geez and Coptic manuscripts, they become incredible. One, from the Abyssinian *Book of the Cock*, tells how Jesus was served a cock cut up and cooked in a dish. Before eating, the Christ blessed the bread and gave it to Judas, who having been "entered" by Satan, left to go home to his wife. Jesus then touched the cock, bringing it to life and telling it to follow Judas and report on his activities.

The cock returns, weeping and telling how Judas' wife urged her husband to betray Jesus and how Judas had arranged with Paul of Tarsus to deliver Jesus into his hands. When the cock ends his account, Jesus releases it to fly for a thousand years in the sky.

Not that Western imaginations were far behind. In medieval sacred legend, in the tales of wanderers like the troubadours, jongleurs, and palmers, in the ballads of the folk, and in the miracle and mystery plays there bloomed a great variety of fanciful Christ legends. *The Croxton Play of the Sacrament,* performed in England sometime after 1461, is characteristic. It tells how a Jewish merchant Jonathas pays a Christian merchant to bring him the Host from the church to find out if it really is God. With his servants, Jonathas abuses the Host, piercing it with a dagger. When it begins to bleed, he tries to throw it into a cauldron of oil. It cleaves to his hand. The servants then nail the Sacrament to a post and try to pull Jonathas' hand from it. His arm comes free, but his hand remains nailed to the post with the Eucharist. Finally, the hand is thrown into the cauldron and the Eucharist into an oven. From the midst of the flames in the oven, Christ appears, bleeding, urging the Jews to repent. He persuades Jonathas to place his maimed arm in the cauldron, whereupon the limb is miraculously restored. Jonathas is convinced, invites the bishop to his home, and decides to be baptized. The Jews, coming in contact with Christ in this fashion, are convinced of his divinity. They are also forgiven.

The Harrowing of Hell is another dramatic illustration. This play, written near the end of the thirteenth century in England, is based on *The Gospel of Nicodemus* and tells of Jesus' descent into Hell to rescue the souls of the just. It is part of that lore which describes the results of an earthquake at Jesus' death which opened the graves out of which many famous saints arose.

Two, Karinus and Leucius, copied down what Jesus did in Hell and, before reentering their graves, left their manuscripts with Annas and Caiaphas so that they could be read to the people.

If one realizes that this sort of thing has been going on for nearly twenty centuries as Christianity has been hard-sold to peoples as disparate as the Goths, the Mohawks, the Japanese, and the Yoruba by missionaries, zealots, and clerks, one also realizes that the "stardust" left by "memories" of the Man from Galilee forms a cosmos of its own with a vastness quite able to boggle mortal minds.

Typical is the effect of Christ's nativity upon the lore of the ox and the ass. Though the canonical gospels mention no animals present near the manger, it took little imagination for the bearers of tradition to infer that oxen were in a stable, that an ass was used to carry the pregnant Mary toward Bethlehem, or even that camels transported the Magi from the East. Ancient Jewish saws encouraged tales about the first two anyhow. Habakkuk proclaims that "He shall lie down betwixt the ox and the ass," while Isaiah affirms the proverb: "the ox knoweth his owner and the ass his master's crib." In fact, so rapidly did these animals associate themselves with the Nativity that in one Coptic text the Virgin bears Christ while Joseph is searching for a midwife. When Joseph returns he finds the new-born babe lying under the careful protection of the ox and ass. Pseudo-Matthew stresses the unusual affection these two animals show for the child, and we have already seen the persistence of the superstition that all cattle will bow down on Christmas Eve to honor the Saviour. In medieval lore, the ass was supposed to have brayed with joy at the news of Christ's birth; the ox, being less emotional, remained quiet. From this belief grew the idea that the ass was a Christian animal and the ox Jewish, even though some legends allow the ox the privilege of accompanying the Holy family into Egypt.

The lore associated with flowers, trees, and shrubs develops in similar fashion. Most common are explanations concerning trees that were cursed for providing the wood for the Cross, like the aspen which trembles forever, the flowering judas which bleeds, the cottonwood which is dwarfed. But there are also trees which are blessed for being used to make the Cross: the elder which is never struck by lightning, the pine which is green all year, paradoxically the trembling aspen which whispers forth the future. Actually, in much medieval art, Christ is crucified not on the dead wood of a tree at all, but on the eternally green foliage of a living plant, most often the Easter lily.

The Chichicastenango Indian version of Christ's biography published by Sol Tax in the *Journal of American Folklore* in 1969 shows how easy it is for the folk mind to mingle the objects of their everyday existence into the episodes of myth.

Jesus Christ was born in the night in Jerusalem, as we know. San José and the Virgin Maria were his parents. They were merchants and they travelled together. They asked many rich people to let them stay in their houses, but the people refused because they thought José and Maria were thieves. Eventually they came to the house of one rich man and asked to stay in their house. They were told that they could not remain there, but they could, if they wished, stay in a stable where the sheep, cows and other animals were kept with their herders. So they went there.

At about 3 A.M., or a little later, when the star Santiago came out, Maria gave birth to a boy with stars on his palms and forehead and who lighted up the world. All of the herders came to see the child, and immediately the owner of the house came.

That night it snowed very hard and the child was very cold, so that it stiffened as if dead. The herders ran for the animals; and the sheep and the cows breathed onto the child's body and warmed it, and the child revived. Then Jesus blessed these animals; but the horses and mules, when they had come, had not believed that the child was God and instead of breathing on him they had eructed at him. God was angry with these animals and said that *they* would never be eaten by man but would have to be beasts of burden always.

Christ preached to all the people who wished to listen, but some were bad and would not hear him. He wandered around and visited 5000 pueblos and 5000 churches and 5000 gardens all over the world. When he encountered a blind man on the road, he told him he would be cured the next day, and the man would be cured; when he met a deaf man, he would tell him that he would hear the next day, and the man would hear.

The Jews were very angry when Christ preached to the people, and they took him to a penitentiary of pure stone—and imprisoned him in a dungeon without light or water. God left his cell, and when the Jews would look in to see if he was still there they saw the light of a firefly, in the dark place, and they thought Jesus was sitting there smoking a cigarette.

After twenty days they no longer saw the firefly, so they thought Jesus was dead. Now Jesus changed the penitentiary into a large church with altars, pine-needles, flowers, *mesetas, idoles,* candles, incense, *santos,* etc., etc. And when the Jews went to the penitentiary to see if Jesus was dead, they saw the church. Maybe this was the first church in the world. The Jews wondered "What are all these things," and were angry and went out to look for Jesus so they could capture him again.

There was a small road in the mountains and God was running on it with the Jews in pursuit when he saw a woman in a house off the road. He asked if he could come in, and the woman said, "With much pleasure" and admitted him. The Jews were coming quickly, and Jesus hurried into the house. There were some chicken eggs in the house and God told the woman he would bless them. He did so, and instantly the eggs were young chickens. He then went outside, where he saw a *ramos* plant and he hid behind the plant; the grass covered him over, so when the Jews came up they couldn't see him.

The Jews came up and asked the woman where Jesus was, saying that they knew that he had passed that way. The woman said that he had passed there twenty days before (arguing to herself that the chickens couldn't have grown so big in less than twenty days). The Jews passed on rapidly.

Then Jesus came from hiding and went again on the road. The Jews came back, and when Jesus saw that they were upon him, he climbed a tree. The Jews had the custom of always looking at the ground: they couldn't look straight ahead or upward; so they did not see Jesus in the tree. But they saw his shadow, and beat it with a stick until they thought they had killed him. Then they passed on.

Jesus came down from the tree and lay down in its shade. Then he blessed the tree that it should serve for cacao. Instantly there was cacao. He told the people (the good Jews who were his followers) that the cacao should serve in *cofradias* in marriages, and for borrowing money and maize. Then the Virgin Maria came up to him, and because Jesus was thirsty she gave him some water in a glass. God blessed the water and it changed into liquor, so that it should serve later for *cofradias*, marriages, money, etc. Then Maria went away.

Jesus began his wanderings, through the towns and mountains, again. The Jews finally found him and put him in the penitentiary. Then they took him from prison and took him to the mountains to make a cross. They came to a large tree from which to make the cross. The Jews began to try to chop the tree down with their axes; but each chip that flew away fell into a spring and became a snake (which came at the feet of the Jews) or a frog, or a toad. These were bad signs for the Jews, and they said that Jesus wouldn't die then. They then asked Jesus to cut the tree himself, and he agreed to do so. With one blow of the ax a chip came off and fell in the water and became a fish (this is why we eat fish during Holy Week). The next chip became a quetzal, a very large one. The next became a large chicken. With each subsequent chip came another food animal.

The tree was finally felled by Jesus, and the Jews made a cross. Jesus had to drag the cross to another place. They stopped on the way to eat. The Jews wrung the neck of the chicken and put it in a pot to cook. They cut off the feet and the wings and they had pure meat, and then they put the chicken in a large leaf with much pepper. Then they sat down to lunch on the chicken, but as they all sat down around the dish the chicken turned to life and scattered the pepper in the eyes of the Jews who were immediately blinded. There were other Jews around, however, and not all were blind, so Jesus did not escape from them. As they walked along again, Jesus bearing the cross, the Jews kept whipping Jesus, and every drop of blood that he bled along the road became an *ocote* tree. There were many cacti in the road, but they parted in Jesus' path.

Finally they came to the spot, and they crucified Jesus. While nailed to the cross, Jesus miraculously turned around completely, exposing his back, and from his back came maize—white, yellow, and black—and beans and potatoes and all the other food plants. Then Jesus died. Jesus was buried. But three days later, a little before 3 A.M. (when the roosters crow) Jesus was resurrected and he went to heaven. There was a large stone over his grave, and Jesus stood on it and with one foot "took off" for heaven. There remained his footprint on the stone.

Jesus stayed three days in heaven, and then he came back to earth to judge the living and the dead. The earth was overturned and the Jews all went to Hell. On earth Jesus ordered *cofradias,* churches, *santos, idoles, costumbres,* marriages, etc., etc., but since all the other people (the Jews) were dead and in Hell, only the Apostles were here to be ordered about. Jesus had a crown of metal thorns. There were no people on earth except the Apostles.

Jesus ordered, when we came, that there be a garden in each of the five thousand pueblos of the world. In one garden he ordered the thirteenth (and lowest) apostle to be the gardener. This gardener's name was Adam. Adam was very sad. The second apostle saw this and asked him if he was happy or sad. Adam said he was sad, because he had no company, such as a woman. The second apostle told Jesus, and Jesus said it would be well to look for a woman for Adam.

Jesus came to earth and made Adam sleep soundly. Jesus and the twelve apostles had a conference. Jesus asked the first apostle what they should do about getting a woman for Adam. The reply was that they should cut some flesh from Adam's palm. Jesus said no, because then Adam would kick her. The third advised that they should take it from Adam's brain and head. No, replied Jesus again, for then the woman would order Adam around. The fourth apostle suggested that they cut a hole in Adam's left chest—the hole to be cut in the shape of the vagina—and take pieces of the heart, lungs, spleen, etc., together with the flesh cut out, to make the woman. It should all be cut out of the left side, because if it were from the right side the woman would be higher and could command the man; the piece of heart should be taken so that the man would have a "good heart" for the woman (i.e., love her and not fight with her). To this all agreed, and Jesus blessed the pieces which had been cut from Adam and laid to his left, and immediately there was a woman.

Jesus told Adam to wake up, and Adam did so, and rose—not knowing from whence came the woman. But he took the woman with him. Jesus told Adam that when in the garden roads, the woman should always walk first. (Today all Indians have their women walking ahead of them.)

In a short time (perhaps three months) the couple saw a snake in the garden. Adam and his wife didn't know what life was; nor did they have clothes.

The snake inserted his tail into the woman's vagina and moved it around, so that the woman felt the tickling there. The woman liked it and wanted it to continue, but the snake said, "No: Adam has one." The woman said to Adam, "Come to me with that!" This was the first time. Later came children, midwives, etc.

When the first child was born, Jesus told them they should baptize it and all future children in the church because the snake had entered the woman first, and it was an animal, and this was bad unless the children were baptized and made Christians. Only when baptized would the children be people (i.e., Christians).

No less incredible is the volume of "fact" and fiction that can assemble about a single explanatory motif connected to such a biography—for example, the "story" behind the Glastonbury hawthorn which blooms each Christmas to honor the Saviour's birth. John Aubrey refers to it in the late seventeenth century in his *Memories of Remarques in Wilts:*

Mr. Anthony Hinton, one of the officers of the Earle of Pembroke, did inoculate, not long before the late civill warres (ten yeares or more), a bud of Glastonbury Thorne, on a thorne, at his farmhouse, at Wilton, which blossoms at Christmas, as the other did. My mother has had branches of them for a flowerpott, several Christmasses, which I have seen. Elias Ashmole, Esq., in his notes upon *Theatrum*

Chymicum, saies that in the churchyard of Glastonbury grew a walnut tree that did putt out young leaves at Christmas, as doth the King's Oak in the New Forest. In Parham Park, in Suffolk (Mr. Boutele's), is a pretty ancient thorne, that blossoms like that at Glastonbury, the people flock hither to see it on Christmas Day. But in the rode that leades from Worcester to Droitwiche is a black thorne hedge at Clayes, half a mile long or more, that blossoms about Christmas Day, for a week or more together. Dr Ezerel Tong sayd that about Rumly-Marsh, in Kent, are Thornes naturally like that near Glastonbury. The soldiers did cutt downe that near Glastonbury; the stump remaines.

and an issue of *The Gentleman's Magazine* early in 1753 tells of the attention such a miracle demands.

Quainton In Buckinghamshire, December 24, 1752. Above 2,000 people came here this night, with lanthorns and candles, to view a black thorn which grows in the neighborhood, and which was remembered (this year only) to be a slip from the famous Glastonbury Thorne, that it always budded on the 24th, was full blown the next day, and went all off at night; but the people, finding no appearance of a bud, 'twas agreed by all, that 25 December, N.S., could not be the right Christmas Day, and accordingly, refused going to Church and treating their friends on that day, as usual; at length the affair became so serious that the ministers of the neighbouring villages, in order to appease the people, thought it prudent to give notice that the old Christmas Day should be kept in as holy as before.

Glastonbury. A vast concourse of people attended the noted thorns on Christmas Eve, New Stile; but, to their great disappointment, there was no appearance of its blowing, which made them watch it narrowly the 5th of Jan., the Christmas Day, Old Style, when it blow'd as usual.

The story of the miracle begins with Joseph of Arimathaea and arrives at Glastonbury "via Robin Hood's barn." Joseph, variously described as a member of the Sanhedrin, as a soldier in Pilate's employ, as a secret follower of Christ, is given credit for taking Jesus' body from the cross and burying it. Tradition feeds this germ until Joseph not only receives and buries the body, but also collects Christ's blood in a grail. He is thrown into prison for his kindness, where Christ appears to him, explains the ritual of burial, and tells him to call the grail "The Chalice."

But tradition doesn't stop there. Other developments are catalogued in a poem written about 1100 or 1200 by a Burgundian Robert de Boron. This poem, often called *The Metrical Joseph,* shoves together accounts of Joseph from various scriptural, apocryphal, and ecclesiastical sources, borrows a scrap or two from Celtic mythology, and displays an insouciance about history worthy of any movie producer. Though he was not the first to do so, de Boron details Joseph's wanderings to the West at the head of a group of Christian exiles and clearly identifies The Chalice which held Christ's blood with the Grail used at the Last Supper. Thus, it is clear the Middle Ages not only gave Joseph of Arimathaea credit for converting much of Western Europe to the True Faith, but also considered Joseph's Chalice and The Grail after which King Arthur's knights quested to be the same dish. This gave Joseph some interesting bedfellows: lustful chaps like Sir Gawain, immaculate fellows like Sir Galahad, unsanctified lovers like Lancelot. It also insured continual and widespread distribution of the story, for few things literary have shown more endurance than the *Arthuriad.*

Just as influential as *The Metrical Joseph,* and a lot more fun, is the romance entitled *The History of the Holy Grail* composed about 1230 by a churchman who had clearly waded through de Boron. It opens with the claim that it is a transcript of a book that Christ Himself had written and then delivered to a hermit who was afflicted with doubts about the Trinity 717 years after the Passion. Roger Loomis, an authority on Arthurian matters, once remarked, "If the claim were true, it would reflect severely not only on the Lord's veracity but also on His talents as a writer of fiction." Loomis goes on to muse whether the account was "the author's private joke, or whether he was touched in the head." In any case, the script was accepted as a serious attempt to present a "reliable background" to the whole matter of the grail. Nonetheless, the information presented scarcely varies from de Boron's poem, although the approach is far more sensational, and dogmatic.

Without getting bogged down, let me stress that it seems to have been important to the author of the *History* that a celibate ecclesiastic and not a married layman have the honor of spreading the Faith westward. As the Joseph of Arimathaea of de Boron was a married layman and as his sidekick and brother-in-law, Bron, to whom Joseph had entrusted the Grail, was also not in orders, a new leader had to be introduced. Who would be more appropriate than Josephes, son of Joseph? Thus, a long passage is devoted to Josephes' spectacular initiation into the rites and secrets of the Eucharist and the episcopacy. Josephes becomes convinced of the Trinity (as well he might) during a celebration of Mass when the bread turns into a child which he is told to cut into three portions and eat. As he swallows, the parts unite. So instructed, Josephes becomes an apostle to the Gentiles, rivaling St. Paul; Bron is downgraded; and Joseph steps aside; Now Josephes assumes care of the Grail and leadership of the mission, and son, father, and uncle-in-law begin the conversion of the western nations. Lands like Sarras, near Egypt; the Orkney Islands; England; Wales; Scotland; and Terre Foraine are brought into the flock by any means available: persuasion, polemics, miracles, military force. When done, the author has accomplished two things: he has filled with "history" the vast chronological gap that lies between the Crucifixion and the Round Table; and he has produced a work that became known throughout Europe as the standard receptacle for information on the grail legend.

The History of the Holy Grail stresses the idea that Joseph's troupe, regardless who was leading it, did actually enter Britain to found the first Christian mission in that "demi-Paradise." Glastonbury was to become the spot. The keepers of the Abbey there had cultivated, at least as early as 1000, the local legend that the first preachers of Christ in Britain had discovered at Glastonbury a church "built by no man's hand" and consecrated to the Virgin herself. In 1184 an old Glastonbury church burned down. The legend was not long in embracing the idea that this now vanished church was the first British church and that twelve disciples of St. Philip and St. James had put it up at the bidding of none other than Archangel Michael.

Still there was no claim that Joseph of Arimathaea was one of those disciples. This claim seems to have come as a "marriage of convenience" when the story of Joseph's efforts to convert the West as told in popular books like de Boron's *The Metrical Joseph* and *The History of the Holy Grail* had to be mated to the details of the local legend. In order that both stories could make sense, it was agreed that Joseph must have been the leader of the twelve disciples who acted at the bidding of Michael. Gradually, Joseph of Arimathaea became one of the main patrons of the monastery. Before long, it seemed likely that he had been buried at this chosen spot. A search was undertaken for his grave. In the fourteenth century a chapel was consecrated to him, a sculpture of the Deposition of Christ was placed on it, and an image of the Virgin was ascribed to his workmanship. People from all over Somerset and "Wessex" began to come to the shrine. Miraculous cures were reported. It also became clearly understood that a hawthorn had sprung out of the staff Joseph had carried out of the Holy Land along with the Grail. Planted near the church, it grew full, miraculously bearing green leaves each Christmas-tide. As John Aubrey and *The Gentleman's Magazine* have reported, even buds and slips from the original thorn have the power. In his little book, *St. Joseph of Arimathaea at Glastonbury*, 1922, the local vicar Lionel S. Lewis writes,

. . . This tree survived the Reformation. Its claims to sanctity awakened the ire of an unhappy Puritan, who expressed himself by diligently and impiously trying to cut it down. It was a gigantic tree for a thorn, and was in two parts. One part he demolished, the other he wounded mortally. And then it revenged itself. A splinter from it flew into his eye and finished him. The wounded tree itself lingered some thirty years—in fact, saw a generation come which hated and revolted from the Puritans—and then died. But in the meantime various thorns were budded from it. One is in the Abbey grounds, a better one in the Parish Churchyard, and a better one still in the Vicarage garden. There are others in various parts. It cannot be struck, but can be budded. Certain it is that it is a Levantine thorn. All botanists agree on this. Certain it is that, in addition to flowering profusely in May, it keeps the habit of blossoming again at Christmas, and nearly always on Christmas Day flowers from it are on the altar of the glorious Parish Church of St. John the Baptist.

Even the ancient folk ballad, "Down in Yon Forest," may be about Joseph and his staff turned tree.

> *Down in yon forest there stands a hall,*
>   *The bells of paradise, I heard them ring;*
> *It's covered all over with purple so tall,*
>   *And I love my Lord Jesus above anything.*
>
> *And in that hall there stands a bed,*
> *It's covered all over with scarlet so red.*
>
> *And by that bedside there lies a stone,*
> *The sweet Virgin Mary a-kneeling thereon.*

And on that bed there lies a knight,
Whose wounds they do bleed by day and by night.

And under that bed there runs a flood,
The one half runs water, the other runs blood.

At the bed's foot there lies a hound,
A-licking the blood as it daily runs down.

At the bed's head there grows a thorn,
Which ever has blossomed since Jesus was born.

At least one hopeful scholar, Anne Gilchrist, has interpreted the knight as Jesus, the hound licking the blood as Joseph, the blossoming thorn as that of Glastonbury.

Finally, mention of church matters in Glastonbury should include the rhyme, "Little Jack Horner," who

Sat in a corner
Eating a Christmas pie;
He put in his thumb
And pulled out a plum
And said what a good boy am I.

English legend insists that the original Jack Horner was actually Thomas Horner, steward to Richard Whiting, the last of the abbots of Glastonbury. At the time that Henry VIII decided to take over whatever Church property he could lay hands to, Whiting is supposed to have sent Horner to London with a Christmas gift intended to appease the greedy king. The gift was a pie in which were secreted the deeds to twelve manorial estates. During the trip, Horner is reported to have opened the pie and seized a juicy deed, the one to the manor of Mells. With this "plum," he established the estate on which his descendants

live till "this very day." Whiting, on the other hand, was ultimately tried by a jury (on which none other than Thomas
Horner sat) for the crime of secreting gold sacramental cups
from the profane touch of the king. Found guilty, he was
hanged, beheaded, and his body quartered in the manner of
the time.

Spun in world enough and time, a folk hero's biography does
develop incredible centrifugal force. British church lore is a
whirling cluster of fantastic accounts known in the Middle Ages
to clerics whose minds dwelt upon the childhood of Jesus. Tales
of how He was scorned by the sons and daughters of rich lords,
how He was berated for having been born next to an ox in a
stable, and how He was ragged in dress were particularly popular. In just about every case, Christ, with the dispatch of the
Rover Boys, is able to confound the rich children by means of
a miracle. So Christ, who is playing in the mud making clay
pigeons, causes them to fly; so He breaks his water jug on the
side of a fountain and quickly makes it whole again; so He
leaps from hill to hill, sits on sunlight, or hangs His pitcher on
a sunbeam. Many times He is cruel, showing the feudal, rather
than the democratic, attitude toward weakness. Not infrequently
His young critics are killed or badly maimed in attempting to
imitate him. The British ballad "The Bitter Withy" is a classic
example of such doings.

> As it befell on a bright holiday,
> Small hail from the sky did fall.
> Our Saviour asked his mother dear
> If he might go and play at ball.
>
> "At ball, at ball, my own dear son,
> It's time that you were gone.
> And don't let me hear of any mischief
> At night when you come home."

So up the hill and down the hill
Our sweet young Saviour run,
Until he met three rich young lords.
Good morning to each one.

"Good morn, good morn, good morn," said they.
"Good morning," then said he,
"And which of you three rich young lords
Will play at ball with me?"

"We are all lords and ladies' sons,
Born in our bower and hall.
And you are nothing but a poor maid's child
Born in an ox's stall."

Sweet Jesus turned him round about;
He did neither laugh nor smile,
But the tears came trickling from his eyes
Like water from the sky.

Then he made him a bridge of the beams of the sun,
And over the water run he;
The rich young lords chased after him
And drowned they were all three.

Then up the hill and down the hill
Three rich young mothers run,
Saying: "Mary mild, fetch home your child,
For ours he's drowned each one."

So Mary mild fetched home her child,
And laid him across her knee,
And with a handful of withy twigs
She give him slashes three.

"Ah, bitter withy, ah, bitter withy,
You've caused me to smart.
And the willow shall be the very first tree
To perish at the heart."

The tale is "an old and antick one," variations of it and its motifs being known all over Eastern and Western folk and popular literature, sometimes with heroes other than Our Lord. It first appears in an interpolated passage in Pseudo-Matthew probably in the fifth century, and related material was still in tradition in Missouri in the twentieth where H. M. Belden met an old Warrensburg Trapper who claimed that

When Jesus was a child he had a brother named Joses, who tho younger was much larger and stronger. Near where they lived were willows, and Joses would tell fibs about Jesus to Mary and then bring willow switches for her to punish him (Jesus) with.

Jesus, the trapper said, got mad at the willow and punished it, supposedly speaking the command, "God rot it!" Ever since the willow brings bad luck, rots quicker than other trees, and if a child is punished with it "he will have much suffering and will die before he is old."

"The Bitter Withy" is interesting in that Mary switches Jesus for his misconduct. In most of the non-canonical accounts, the Virgin is quite in awe of her Son. Gordon Gerould, the Princeton professor who spent a lot of hours over "The Bitter Withy," emphasized that "Indeed, in all the versions of the Childhood from both the Continent and England that I have read, the Mother's attitude toward her Son is one of respected adoration." But such has not always been the case. Though Mary is to learn that she cannot interfere with Jesus as He goes "about His Father's business," she acts like any other mother in a few legends. At the west end of the Cathedral of Lucca in Italy, there is an exterior fresco which shows the Virgin whipping Christ with a rod. Jesus is entreating his grandmother, St. Anna, to intercede. After Christ is punished in these stories, he is apt to be a bit spiteful, and a number of plants and trees which "allowed" their branches to be used have suffered eternal fates like that of the withy.

Mary can be spiteful, too. In the ballad "The Holy Well" she reacts furiously to the scorning of her cub and her wrath is stayed only by Jesus' sweetness and Gabriel's tolerance.

> As it fell out on a May morning
> And on a bright holiday,
> Sweet Jesus asked his mother dear
> If he might go to play.
>
> "To play, to play, sweet Jesus shall go,
> And to play now get you gone,
> And let me hear of no complaint
> Tonight when you come home."
>
> Sweet Jesus went to yonder town
> As far as the holy well,
> And there he did see as fine children
> As any tongue can tell.
>
> He said: "God bless you every one,
> May Christ your portion be;
> Little children shall I play with you
> And you shall play with me."
>
> But they did jointly answer, "No,
> For we're lords and ladies' sons
> And you are but a mean mother's child
> Born in an ox's stall."
>
> Sweet Jesus turned himself around
> And neither did laugh nor smile,
> But the tears came trickling from his eyes
> Like water from the sky.

Sweet Jesus turned himself around
To his mother's home went he.
He says, "I've been down in yonder town
As far as you can see.

"I have been down to yonder town
As far as the holy well,
And there did see as fine children
As any tongue can tell.

"I bid God bless them every one
And Christ their portion be;
I asked them should I play with them,
And they should play with me.

"They quickly turned and answered, 'No,
We're lords and ladies all
And you are but mild Mary's child
Born in an ox's stall.' "

"Well, if you are mild Mary's child
Born in an ox's stall
You're God the King all over them
You can reign above them all.

"Go down, go down to yonder town
As far as the holy well,
And take away those sinful souls
And dip them all in Hell."

"No, no" sweet Jesus smiled and said
"No, no that cannot be.
There are too many sinful souls
Crying out for help of me."

Then up and spoke the angel Gabriel
Upon a good set steven, [steady voice]
"Although you're but a maiden's child,
You are the King of heaven."

But she is a good mother. One tale, called "The Seven Virgins" in its ballad form, tells of her trip to Calvary, where she goes accompanied by seven lovely maids in order to comfort her dying Son. A British chapbook printer felt it appropriate to round off his version of the story with the request: "God give us grace in our place/To pray for Victoria our Queen."

Still, as one granny-woman in the southern hills said, "the touchingest ballet of them all" is "The Cherry-Tree Carol." It's based on a miracle recounted in Pseudo-Matthew XX as occurring during the third day of the flight into Egypt. Mary, feeling the heat, tells Joseph she is going to have to rest under a palm. As she relaxes, she looks up at the tree and sees it full of fruit. "I want some," she tells Joseph, who abruptly points out that the fruit is too high for anyone to pick and what she really wants is water anyhow. Jesus, sitting on his Mother's lap, hears the exchange and orders the palm to bend down. The tree complies, laying its topmost branches directly at Mary's feet.

As this story wanders north, entering art, poetry, song, and story, the tree and the fruit change with the climate, becoming the fig, the apple, the cherry. In Catalan, Spain, and Provencal, France the miracle occurs on the trip from Nazareth to Bethlehem, where the couple encounters a gardener in an apple tree. Mary asks for an apple, and the gardener tells her she can pick one for herself. Joseph tries to get one for her, but the branches rise out of his reach. When Mary tries, they bow down. In Britain, where the tree is almost always a cherry, Christ may still be in the womb when Mary asks for the fruit and He either gives the tree instructions from there or miraculously appears on Mary's lap to give the order. In one of the Coventry mystery plays, it is not even the season for fruit, and Joseph, seeing a cherry, tells Mary that at another time of year she might "feed thereon" her fill.

Mary replies,

Turn again, husband, and behold yon tree:
How that it blooms now so sweetly.

Joseph hardly notices and tells her to "come along" or they are
going to be late arriving in the city. However, she is insistent:

Now, my spouse, I pray you to behold
How the cherries are grown upon yon tree,

adding,

For to have thereof right fain I would.

He says that the tree is high and the task of getting the fruit a
tough one. "Therefore," he suggests,

Let him pluck you cherries who begat you with child.

At this point Mary decides to consult the Lord Himself,

Now, good Lord, I pray thee grant me this boon,
To have of these cherries, be it your will.

Though there are no stage directions indicating it, the cherry
tree obviously bends over, for Mary completes her speech,

Now, I thank it God, this tree boweth to me down!
I may now gather enough and eat my fill.

The miracle is impressive to Joseph who bewails the fact he has
"offended my God's Trinity" speaking to his spouse "these un-
kind words." He concludes that Mary is bearing "the king's son
of bliss," pointing out that "He will help us in our need." Mary
is utterly tolerant, thanking her husband for his remarks and

suggesting they "forth wend." "The Father Almighty," she says as they leave, "he be our comfort! The Holy Ghost glorious he be our friend!"

Ballad singers in Virginia are familiar with a similar dialogue:

> As Mary and Joseph were walking the green,
> Said Mary to Joseph, so mild and serene,
> "Joseph, pull me a cherry, I am surely with child."
>
> Said Joseph to Mary, so stubborn and unkind,
> "Let the father of your baby pull cherries for you."

In Kentucky, the ballad also tells of Joseph's remorse for doubting Mary, and he gets down on his hands and knees before her begging her forgiveness. In some texts, he even asks the child when His birthday will be. Jesus, who is either in the womb or a mere infant at breast, names Old Christmas Day and may take it upon Himself to foretell the story of his life to come.

> Then Mary took her young son
> And set him on her knee:
> "I pray thee now, dear child,
> Tell how this world shall be."
>
> "O I shall be as dead, mother,
> As the stones in any wall;
> O the stones in the street, mother,
> Shall mourn for me all.
>
> "And upon a Wednesday
> My vow I will make,
> And upon Good Friday
> My death I will take.
>
> "Upon Easter-day, mother,
> My rising shall be;

O the sun and the moon
Shall uprise with me.

"The people shall rejoice,
And the birds they shall sing,
To see the uprising
Of the heavenly king."

Herod's anguish over the coming of a "heavenly king" is almost as popular a theme as Joseph's doubt concerning Mary. Two ballads, "The Carnel and the Crane" and the briefer "St. Stephen and Herod," cover the King's confusion. Herod is in his chamber when he notices that "a star in the east land" is shedding its light directly in his window. When he tries to get an explanation for this near-impertinence, either Stephen, who is a stablehand, or the Wise Men inform him that "a princely babe" that "no king can destroy" has been born "that night." Herod scoffs. "If this is true," he replies, "this cock in this roasting dish will rise and speak." With that the cock leaps to its feet and crows, *Christus natus est!* In the longer ballad, the King then orders all children under two slain. They are brought to him impaled on spears, but Jesus is not among them. Mary and Joseph have fled with Him toward Egypt, where they experience a varied group of miracles, the best known being the one of the husbandman. This farmer is sowing his seed as the Family passes. Jesus tells him to fetch his ox and wagon because, if he'll check, he'll find his seed is now corn full grown. When Herod, pursuing, arrives, the husbandman is able to say that Jesus did pass by, but it was during the time when the seed was being sowed. Herod noting the full grown crop figures that Christ had passed nine months earlier and (rather naively) turns back discouraged. The story exists all over Europe and, as we have seen, in Mexico as well, sometimes with Joseph or Mary setting the miracle into motion.

Such is the stuff that folk biographies are made of. In Christian tradition, "the stardust of the memory" literally "haunting the reveries" of the Western world, forming and reforming, to verify an ethic that has served the purposes of souls as faith-full as St. Jerome, Henry VIII, and Billy Sunday, its influences on the mid-winter rites rivaled only by "the melody" associated with Nicholas, called Santa Claus.

4

SANCT HERR 'CHOLAS

JAMES H. Barnet, who has published a useful book on the American Christmas, quotes a news account that appeared in *P.M.* on December 24, 1947. It seems a war orphan living in an institution wrote Santa Claus asking that "a real home" be found for him. The orphanage, "intercepting" the letter, publicized the affair with comments such as "we've just got to find a home or deny the Santa Claus legend." Supposedly, over 100 families indicated willingness to take the child. Such accounts, along with reports of dying children who have been visited by Santa Claus in September, October, or even June because they could not live till late December, of hardbitten soldiers playing Santa to captured enemy youngsters, of homeless families who appealed to Santa to help them relocate, all testify to the power of our belief that people have an innate right to be visited by Santa Claus and that no effort to protect this right is too great to make. In fact, from 1914 to 1928, when it was investigated unfavorably by the postal authorities, a Santa Claus Association founded by John D. Gluck was not only able to flourish in New York City but was even copied in other towns.

Its purpose: to get letters addressed to Santa Claus from the
post offices, investigate the circumstances of the children involved, and do for the youngsters whatever was expected from
the "jolly old elf." Even the law has fallen in line. Barnet cites
a 1936 ruling by Judge Michael A. Musmanno of the Alle-
gheny County Criminal Court in Pennsylvania that held
doubters of Santa Claus in contempt. This is the same gentleman who later was to take umbrage at the fact Scandinavian
Lief Ericsson might have beaten Italian Cristoforo Columbo to
America. He also cites an opinion handed down by Judge John
Hatcher of the West Virginia Supreme Court which included
this grammatically shaky, but sentimentally sound, assertion:
"Let legislation outlaw the law of evolution, if they must; let the
Constitution be amended till it looks like a patchwork quilt; but
rob not childhood of its most intriguing mystery—Santa Claus."

To be sure, there have been antagonists. Here and there a
psychiatrist has argued that the "sugar-daddy" concept of Santa
Claus has impaired American youngsters' ability to think real-
istically and to cope with necessity. When Christ and His Virgin
Mother have found themselves elbowed out the church door by
the red-suited elf, a minister or two has warned his congregation
that "Santa is crowding Christ from our lives," that "reindeer
are replacing the ox and the ass by the crèche," that "St.
Nicholas is a form of Anti-Christ." Perhaps, a nadir, or is it
apogee, was reached in Fort Lauderdale in the fall of 1971 when
Santa, stepping from his inevitable helicopter at a supermarket,
was knocked to the ground by screaming kiddies (many of them
with driver's licenses) and deftly relieved of his presents.

The turmoil has attracted the sharks. There is no point
lingering on a description of the "kids from one to ninety-two"
Christmas created by our merchants and advertisers. From that
mid-fall day, sometimes as early as Martinmas, when Santa rear-
rives; through the comic-strip gags, the encounters with rented

red suits lobby after street corner, and the presents selected by
the recipient; to those postholiday exchanges "for something
more suitable, you do understand," our public has been instructed how grotesque the "unbirthday" can be. And a town in
Indiana callously changes its name to Santa Claus, erects a
statue to him, and booming commercially remails bags of
letters "now properly canceled." And Jewish Irving Berlin
waxes rich on dreams of a "White Christmas." And Mommy is
caught red-handed, kissing Santa Claus. And Dennis the Menace
sits atop a pile of toys as high as the tree itself asking two
harried adults, "Is this all?" While Everyman wonders, will
commerce, who has ruined our little faith, ruin our little hope
and charity to boot?

Nicholas, the saint who started all this, is a genuine folk figure. Everything we know about him comes to us through oral
tradition, the first written legends having been transcribed
about 500 years, twenty generations, after his death. One of the
earliest to record facts about Nicholas was Methodius, a ninth-
century patriarch of Constantinople, who tells us that the
Saint was born in Patara, a town named after one of Apollo's
sons. The date given is "sometime near the end of the third to
the beginning of the fourth centuries"; the location is Lycia,
Asia Minor, what is now southwestern Turkey. Except for the
fact he was probably Bishop of Myra during the reign of
Diocletian, was imprisoned to be released when Constantine
came to the throne, we really know nothing about him—so
little, in fact, that in 1969 the Pope made his anniversary celebration optional for Roman Catholics and dropped his Day
from the Calendar.

Nonetheless, we are assured he was an only son, of parents
who were widely known for their good deeds and kindly manners, and (like a true folk hero) gave early manifestations of his
pious nature, even observing the prescribed fast days by reject-

ing his mother's breast during infancy. Later, upon receiving his quite considerable inheritance, he is said to have spent it all to help the wretched. The most persistent legend about this side of his personality is also set in the early years. It seems there was a noble family whose fortune had been lost. The three virtuous daughters resolved to recoup these losses for the beloved papa by selling their bodies and, to be sure, souls. Nicholas prevented this catastrophe. Three nights in succession he threw bags of gold from the street into the girls' home, changing poverty to wealth, allowing virtue to take a firm stand. Because of this, three bags of gold have symbolized his name and role, and the tale has grown up that the money was tossed down the smoke-hole where it landed in stockings which the girls had hung by the "chimney" to dry.

Before long this good man becomes involved in miracles. Designated by God to fill the Archbishop's See (the Good Lord intervened in the dispute among the aspiring bishops), Nicholas was at once faced with a crisis. A woman, excited by her chance to see a Heaven-selected archbishop, rushed forth forgetting her baby who was sitting in a pot over the fire waiting to be bathed. Suddenly remembering, she implored the passing celebrity "to do something." Nicholas bade her return home, where she discovered the child unharmed playing with the bubbles in the boiling water. He makes the Sign of the Cross over an uncontrollable child, driving the evil from his body; he restores to life three scholars whose bodies were hacked to bits and stored in pickle barrels by an innkeeper who had murdered and robbed them; he quiets storms so that sailors will return safely to harbor. The most famous miracle of all involved a great famine that swept the land. As men, women, and children starved, Bishop Nicholas went down to the docks and approached the grain ships as they stopped off en route to Alexandria. Beseeching each to unload a portion of its cargo to relieve the hun-

ger of his people, he promised the sailors that whatever had been
removed would be restored by the time they arrived at their
destination. Not only did the grain on the ships miraculously
refill the holds during the sail toward Alexandria, but the un-
loaded portions increased sufficiently to feed everyone for two
years. As the evidence from this miracle came in, Bishop
Nicholas gained a large number of immediate converts. Later
he takes on the Goddess Diana, who was sufficiently irritated
by his success in weaning followers from her shrine that she
assumed the form of a nun and gave some sailors a magic oil
which they were to spread on the steps and walls of Nicholas'
monastary, supposedly as a holy offering. Nicholas took one look
at the oil and told the sailors to spread it on the open waters
instead. It soon burst into all-consuming flames.

It is only natural that such a man be reported among the dis-
cussants at Nicaea in 325, when the first ecumenical council
of the Church was held. In spite of the fact his name does not
appear on the lists of those attending this Council and is not
mentioned by a single ancient historian, Nicholas is deemed
to have been the most honored churchman there and to have
taken a lead in quashing the heresy of Arius, that priest who
maintained Christ and God were not of the same substance.

His death date has become fixed on December 6, 342, and he
seems to have recited Psalm 11 ("In the Lord I put my trust")
with his very last breath. Holy Angels transported his soul to
Heaven. An oil with curative powers began to flow from his
tomb. By the ninth century he had been canonized and was on
his way to becoming the patron of lands as various as Russia,
Greece, Germany, Austria, Belgium, France, the Netherlands,
and Sicily; of people as unharmonious as thieves and children,
sailors and virgins. Pilgrimages to his tomb and its ever-flowing
curative oil became fashionable. His images, his pictures, his
relics became sacred. Tales abounded telling how the curative

oil ceased one day when an innocent archbishop was exiled by a jealous ruler, only to start again when the archbishop was recalled; how dead men, missing children, stolen relics were restored; how Satan was confounded or the sick cured; how villains, pagans, even the Jews were converted by miracles involving his image.

In Jacobus de Voragine's *The Golden Legend or Lives of the Saints as Englished by William Caxton* this last sure-fire subject is illustrated. It seems a man borrowed "of a Jew a sum of money, and sware upon the altar of S. Nicholas that he would render and pay it again as soon as he might, and gave none other pledge." The man kept the money so long the Jew got impatient and went to court to collect. Before the trial, the debtor took the money he owed and put it inside a golden staff. Just before he took his oath to tell nothing but the truth, he asked the Jew to hold the staff and then swore he had already delivered "more than he ought." Next he asked for the staff back, received it from the innocent Jew, and went away exonerated. He hadn't gone far when he became sleepy and lay down in the road, the staff beside him. Along came "a cart with four wheels" and "slew him, and brake the staff with gold that it spread abroad." When the Jew heard about the accident, he went to the scene and saw how he had been defrauded. The onlookers told him he should take the gold, that it was rightfully his. However, he refused, saying, "But if he that was dead were not raised again to life by the merits of S. Nicholas, he would not receive it, and if he came again to life, he would receive baptism and become Christian." The dead man immediately arose, and the Jew, good to his word, was converted. Perhaps it is appropriately ironic that Nicholas' three golden balls frequently end up above the shops of money-changers, pawnbrokers, and usurers—"the Jewish trades" as they have been called.

The oldest known monument to the worship of this versatile

Saint is the Church of St. Priscus and St. Nicholas built in Constantinople by Justinian in the sixth century. By 679 his fame had spread west and there was a shrine at St. Amandus fifty miles from Liège, France. Legend reports that in 1087 forty-seven Italian merchants and clerics were able to overpower four monks and steal the Saint's remains, transporting them from Myra to Apulia in Italy, and by 1100 the Church of St. Nicholas at Bari, Apulia, had become the shrine to which pilgrimages for St. Nicholas were made. Bari, which was strongly Norman French in culture, drew pilgrims and converts from all over Western Europe. Furthermore, as a patron of sailors, especially Norman sailors, Nicholas' reputation found a home in every port. And when the boatmen of the Scheldt, Meuse, and Moselle rivers adopted him from their seafaring brothers, his fame gained steady access to the hinterlands. Mary Sinclair Crawford, who did a study of Robert Wace's long poem about Nicholas, cites numerous liturgical dramas, *lectiones,* and sermons about the Saint. At one point she states that "no fewer than 527 Latin hymns were composed and sung in his honor." There may be long gaps in the story, but there is no doubt by the Middle Ages St. Nicholas and his death day, December 6, were honored by the people of the West, his role as protector of the downtrodden and the desperate as necessary to the Scheme of Things as that of the Virgin Mother herself.

Quite illustrative is his "sponsorship" of the Boy Bishop or Nicholas Bishop ceremony in the medieval church schools. Held December 5, this "king for a day" rite was ancestor to the modern custom of letting some Boy Scout take over as mayor of the city, although the event was a bit more vigorous "in the old age." Outright rebellion against the authorities, parody of matters held sacred, and the general temper of "the panty raid" prevailed. The mock Bishop was dressed handsomely like the real thing, and he led his companions in a "solemn" procession,

in some cities actually being allowed possession of the church.
There was food, drink, and riot for the adult onlookers; food,
less drink, and sport for the students—and release for all, even
the royalty. Conrad I of Germany tells how he had his retinue
throw apples down a monastary aisle during one Boy Bishop
parade only to be astounded that the youngsters could maintain
their composure in the turmoil. The revel died out in the sixteenth century, although some West County schools in England
were allowing the boys to get drunk at their Master's cellar or
to bring "a Barrell of good Ale" into the chapel itself as late
as 1920.

It is, then, small wonder that the Viking cathedral in Green-
land is dedicated to St. Nicholas, that Columbus dedicated a
port in Haiti to him, that the Spaniards named the town we call
Jacksonville, Florida, after him—or that today, as Professor
Charles W. Jones once reminded the New-York Historical
Society,

In Wales and Crete, he is invoked by fishermen. In Southampton
and Tripoli, he guards sailors and merchants. In Russia, he still
protects communists from wolves. In Poland and France, he brings
husbands and babies home. In Aberdeen and Bologna, he gives
passing marks to college students.

Nor is the evolution of this patron figure into a "jolly old elf"
with woolly, red suit and "jelly-jiggling tummy" as far-fetched
as one might suspect, although the process is long and confusing.
It involves two major desires and a willingness: the desire of the
Roman Catholics not to credit any Saturnalian sprite with the
mid-winter dispensation of gifts when a good saint like Martin
or Nicholas is both available and already associated with gift-
giving; the desire of the Protestants not to credit any Roman
Catholic saint with the mid-winter dispensation of gifts if some
local, albeit once pagan, sprite is both available and already

associated with gift-giving; and the willingness of both groups to accept El Niño Jesus as the dispenser in spite of the fact He was traditionally the recipient of whatever was being offered. The result of this urge-counterurge is a mosaic of beliefs, manners, and dates that not only varies from land to land but from hearth to hearth within the lands.

It surely would have made sense had all gift-giving duties been conferred upon the Christ-child and all pagan sprites and Christian saints dismissed. But precision was not what the Church wanted in the early days. We've already seen that the Roman Catholic method had never been to eliminate pagan ritual or even change the time of pagan worship, but rather to allow the converts to continue what heathenish practices were dear to them, requiring only that the symbols and names of the Christian deities be introduced. Because of this leniency, bunny rabbits and colored eggs have become associated with Easter, hearts and flowers with St. Valentine, yule logs and mistletoe with Christmas. Thus, as Western Europe converted, the custom of exchanging gifts was set not only on November 11, with St. Martin the dispenser, but also on December 6, with St. Nicholas as the dispenser—the date varying with the climate, local adaptations of the Roman mid-winter rites, and ecclesiastical whim.

At the same time, the pre-Christian sprites, Roman and Teutonic, continued to flourish in spite of the saintly substitutes. These elfin gift-givers and keepers of conduct, which author Francis X. Weiser once grouped under the rather paleontological term "Christmas Man," were cultivated by the Protestants in their issue with anything Papist. One such "Christmas Man" was the ancient Roman Befana, that genial hag who searches the world leaving candy and sweets for good children, stones and charcoal for the bad. In spite of the fact she was active for centuries before Jesus, Christians claim she was a hussy who refused to go with the Magi to see the Christ Child

because she had too much housework to do and who, changing
her mind, was unable to catch up. She now searches the world
each Epiphany Eve looking for the Holy Infant. Another was
the disheveled, hook-nosed Berchta who checks the cleanliness
and industry of Germanic children during the Twelfth Night
period, looking especially for dirty barns and sloppy spinning.
Most important was Knecht Ruprecht, a skin- or straw-clad
spirit "who's going to find out who's naughty or nice" and
give the nice ones gifts. Obviously a refugee from heathen
ritual, Knecht Ruprecht has been closely associated with
Nicholas in many areas, sometimes accompanying the Saint as
"Black Pete," a terrible assistant with a dingy face, horns, a
long red tongue, fiery eyes, and chains that clank—a fellow
easily seen as Beelzebub himself. Bad children are saved from
Black Pete's clutches only by the intervention of the kindly
Nicholas, who may well tolerate the association so that he, in
the fashion of Shakespeare's Prince Hal, "may be more wondered at." Ruprecht-like figures have a myriad of forms and go
under names such as Krampus, Grampus, or Bartel and often
are fused with the Saint, creating semichurch, semipagan figures
like Ru Klaus (Rough Nicholas), Pelznickel (Furry Nicholas),
and Aschenklas (Ash Nicholas).

Thus, it is not hard to see why in, say, the Dutch ceremony
the children wait the coming of Sanct Herr Nicholaas or
Sintirklass on December 6 by placing their wooden shoes near
the fire and leaving a generous portion of hay for his handsome
horse. After nightfall, the Saint, dressed in the red robes of a
bishop, appears in the sky riding a white steed and followed by
the dark-skinned Pete. On his back are three bags, once full of
gold for those desperate virgins in Asia Minor, now packed with
goodies. The horse alights on the rooftops, Black Pete descends
the chimney and fills the shoes of deserving youngsters with
candy, cookies, and sweetmeats. For the bad children, at the

Saint's instruction, he leaves a birch-rod to symbolize both his displeasure and the fate they can now expect. The next morning the parents get into the act and the standard mid-winter indulgences of the pagan, agricultural peoples are perpetrated through overdrinking, overeating, merriment, and appropriately regulated escapades of sex. Nor is there reason to be surprised if, in another land, the figure accompanying St. Nicholas is St. Peter, Gabriel himself, or a sweet girl dressed in white vaguely reminiscent of a less attractive Befana; or if the date is December 25 or January 1; or even if the date is November 11 and the figure called Pelzmartin (Furry Martin).

In today's America and through American enthusiasm in many parts of today's Europe, the idea of shoes and stockings as receptacles for small, simple presents brought by St. Nicholas to reward good people has combined with the idea of the Christkind (Kriss Kringle) arranging other offerings about the crèche or under the Teutonic *tannenbaum,* the elfin figure is known as Santa Claus, and the date is fixed as Christ's Mass. This pattern began to harden in the nineteenth century, in New York City, rather arbitrarily and rather whimsically. Washington Irving had something to do with it all.

Irving, who delighted in sketching warm, satiric vignettes of the burghers who once inhabited Nieuw Amsterdam, let his whimsy and artistic talent play with the Dutch saint, Nicholas, in Diedrich Knickerbocker's *A History of New York* of 1809.

Nor must I omit to record one of the earliest measures of this infant settlement, inasmuch as it shows the piety of our forefathers, and that, like good *Christians,* they were always ready to serve GOD after they had first served themselves. Thus, having quietly settled themselves down and provided for their own comfort, they bethought themselves of testifying their gratitude to the great and good *St. Nicholas* for his protecting care in guiding them to this delectable abode. To this end they built a fair and goodly chapel within the fort, which they consecrated to his name; whereupon he immediately took the town of New Amsterdam under his peculiar patronage, and he has ever since been and I devoutly hope will ever be, the tutelar saint of this excellent city. At this early period was instituted that pious ceremony, still religiously observed in all our ancient families of the right breed, of hanging up a stocking in the chimney on *St. Nicholas* eve; which stocking is always found in the morning miraculously filled—for the good *St. Nicholas* has ever been a great giver of gifts, particularly to children. . . .

—and as of yore, in the better days of man, the deities were wont to visit him on earth and bless his rural habitations, so, we are told, in the sylvan days of New Amsterdam, the good St. Nicholas would often make his appearance in his beloved city, of a holiday afternoon, riding jollily among the tree-tops, or over the roofs of the houses, now and then drawing forth magnificent presents from his breeches-pockets, and dripping them down the chimneys of his favorites. Whereas, in these degenerate days of iron and brass, he never shows us the light of his countenance, nor ever visits us, save one night in the year, when he rattles down the chimneys of the descendants of patriarchs, confining his presents merely to the children, in token of the degeneracy of the parents.

Actually, there are about two dozen references to St. Nicholas in the Knickerbocker history, including the famous attitude: "laying a finger beside his nose" before his departure into the sky.

Twenty-six years later, still fascinated by his own fanciful pictures of Dutch colonial life, Irving helped start a St. Nicholas Society. Charles W. Jones, researching a speech that was to be delivered before the New-York Historical Society, found little or no evidence that there was a true "St. Nicholas cult" in pre-English New York. "Without Washington Irving," he concluded, "there would be no Santa Claus." "Santa Claus," he continues, "was *made* by Washington Irving. As if that were not enough, his partner and brother-in-law, James K. Paulding, who could not leave a good joke alone, repeated it again and again." The works of both men were widely read during the nineteenth century, and Paulding's *The Book of St. Nicholas,* which was full of coined St. Nicholas materials such as "The Revenge of St. Nicholas" and "The Ride of St. Nicholas on New Year's Eve," was most successful. Jones may well be right, but Irving wasn't working off as little Dutch lore as the Historical Society speech would have one think. He certainly never *made* Santa Claus in the way Charles Schulz *made* Charlie Brown's "The Great Pumpkin."

There seems little doubt that Dutch children awaited the arrival of St. Nicholas on December 6 in Nieuw Amsterdam as their parents had done in Oud. It is also a fact that other Colonial groups knew of him and associated him with gift-giving on that date, on the twenty-fifth, or at New Year's. A woodcut preserved on an 1810 broadside which was printed on commission for the New-York Historical Society shows what he must have "looked like" in Dutch days. He stands proud and tall, wearing bishop's robes, holding a purse in one hand and a birch rod in the other, accompanied by a beehive and a dog that looks like a cat. Beside him, like characters in a medieval morality play, are pictured two children on a mantel. One is a Good, Happy Child, cherubic with a stocking full of presents. The other is a Bad, Sad Child, spiteful with a switch as boutonnière and a stocking full of birch rods. A verse, questionable in its altruism, accompanies the engravings:

> *Saint Nicholas, my dear good friend*
> *To serve you ever was my end.*
> *If you will, me something give,*
> *I'll serve you ever while I live.*

Noticeably lacking is Black Pete, who seems to have failed to survive the transatlantic journey.

Other things would fail to survive too. The bishop's red robe would give way to a fur-trimmed suit; the erect, saintly stature would sag to jolly rotundity; the single white steed would be replaced by eight, finally nine, reindeer; the permanent address would read the North Pole rather than the Celestial City, and all comings and goings would be commerce. The author of the poem we usually call "The Night Before Christmas" and the German-born illustrator, Thomas Nast, effected most of this utter transformation.

"The Night Before Christmas," actually titled "An Account of a Visit from St. Nicholas," was first published anonymously in the Troy (New York) *Sentinel* on December 23, 1823, and was prefaced with a note by the editor, Orville L. Holley, setting the scene:

We know not to whom we are indebted for the following description of that unwearied patron of music—that homely and delightful personage of parental kindness, Santa Claus, his costumes, and his equipage, as he goes about visiting the firesides of this happy land laden with Christmas bounties; but from whomsoever it may have come, we give thanks for it. There is, to our apprehension, a spirit of cordial goodness in it, a playfulness of fancy and a benevolent alacrity to enter into the feelings and promote the simple pleasures of children which are altogether charming. . . .

Clement Clarke Moore, born in 1779 son of the clergyman who gave communion to Alexander Hamilton as he lay dying after his duel with Aaron Burr, is now consistently credited as author. Moore, a professor "of Biblical learning and interpretation of Scripture" in New York City, may not deserve the honor. The chances are excellent it should go to a sometime major in the Revolution, land surveyor, and "renaissance man" from Dutchess County, Henry Livingston, Jr. (1748–1828). Most people who have taken time to look into this scholarly enigma agree that Harriet Butler, the eldest daughter of a Troy clergyman, heard Dr. Moore read the poem at his home, probably before Christmas Day in 1822, was sufficiently entranced to copy it down in her album and to give it to Holley for publication the following fall. The mystery lies in where Dr. Moore got the verse he read.

"An Account of a Visit from St. Nicholas" was not publicly claimed by Moore until 1844 when he included it in a volume of thirty-seven verses, prefacing the collection with the statement that all but two, attributed to his wife, were "written by me." Twenty-one have subtitles telling why he wrote them; nine, including "The Night Before Christmas" have no subtitles at all. And while one doesn't like to question the veracity of a professor of "Scriptural interpretation," the anthology itself clearly indicates that Moore was not in fact the author of at least five of the thirty-five verses he claimed, two being assigned by their own subtitles to William Bard and P. Hone and three being direct translations of Italian and Greek works. What the good professor meant by "written by me" is moot. Perhaps, in the fashion of country singers, he felt anything he revised or touched up could be classified as his. Or perhaps he felt that works he had read, and so interpreted, and called "favorites" were written by him in some sentimental way. When he was eighty-three years old and one year away from death, he was interviewed as to the authorship of the poem. Then he said that "a portly rubicund Dutchman, living in the neighborhood of his father's country seat, Chelsea, suggested to him the idea of making St. Nicholas the hero of the Christmas piece," and that Miss Butler had not received her copy of the poem from him, but rather from a transcript made by one of his "female relatives." He also remarked that he had written the poem forty years before for his "two children." However, the fact that Dr. Moore had three children in 1822 makes the whole pattern of his recollection suspect.

To be sure, Livingston's descendants were (and are) convinced that Moore did not compose the poem and that "what really happened" is recorded in an old letter from Elizabeth Livingston Montgomery, though the scholarly detective finds it delicate to explain why Moore, who was unmarried and perhaps twenty-five years old, should be employing a governess for "his children."

The little incident connected with the first reading of "A Visit from St. Nicholas" was related to me by my grandmother, Catherine Breese, the eldest daughter of Henry Livingston. As I recollect her story there was a young lady spending the Christmas holidays with the family at Locust Grove. On Christmas morning Mr. Livingston came into the dining-room, where the family and their guests were just sitting down to breakfast. He held the manuscript in his hand and said that it was a Christmas poem he had written for them. He then sat down at the table and read aloud to them "A Visit from St. Nicholas." All were delighted with the verses and the guest in particular, was so much impressed by them that she begged Mr. Livingston to let her have a copy of the poem. He consented and made a copy in his own hand, which he gave to her. On leaving Locust Grove, when her visit came to an end, this young lady went directly to the home of Clement C. Moore, where she filled the position of governess to his children.

The truth probably is that Moore heard verses about a visit from St. Nicholas somehow, somewhere, perhaps from the "Dutch gardener," perhaps in his twenties from a governess or guest. He probably reworked these verses, possibly adding enough that he came to think of them as his own. Probably the original from which he worked and which had come to him via the gardener or "young lady" was a poem by Henry Livingston, Jr. Certainly, Livingston makes a better father for this particular brainchild than Moore. Moore was a learned, ponderous man, "educated for the church," with a limited penchant for gaiety, while Livingston was a whimsical chap who once switched the lyrics in his music book from "God Save the King" to "God Save Congress" and who produced a steady stream of light, occasional verse, much of it in the same meter as "The Night Before. . . ."

> *To my dear brother Beekman: I sit down to write,*
> *Ten minutes past eight and a very cold night.*
> *Not far from me sits, with a baullancy cap on,*
> *Our very good cousin, Elizabeth Tappan.*

Legends attributing "An Account of a Visit from St. Nicholas" to "their Henry" abound in the Livingston family. They tell how the poem was "first read to the children at the old homestead below Poughkeepsie" in about 1804 or 1805; how long ago "my brother, in looking over his papers, found the original"; how the treasured manuscript was destroyed in a Wisconsin fire in 1847 or 1848; how astonished everyone was when the poem was attributed to Dr. Moore; and how, in the 1860's, when one of the men in the family was teaching at Churchill's Academy at Sing Sing, he had a violent dispute with one of Clement Moore's grandsons over the authorship of the poem.

Surely whatever fame awaits Moore or Livingston at the solution of the mystery rests not on the merit of the poem but on its position as a perennial commonplace. Nonetheless, this indefatigable popularity was slow in developing, the momentum generating from its inclusion in widely selling anthologies of "literature by Americans" like Griswold's 1849 anthology of verse or the Duyckinck *Cyclopaedia of American Literature* of 1855 and in a host of post-Civil War school readers and holiday supplements, reaching some sort of dizziness in annual costumed readings such as those conducted by Newport socialite James Van Alen, who has even added seventeen couplets of his own composition "to make the fun last longer."

Besides doing much to solidify the idea of St. Nicholas as gift-giver, the Moore-Livingston poem helped fix two major modifications in the legend. First, it reduced the Saint in size, changing him from a tall, stately patron to an elf, trimming his red bishop's robes with white fur and giving him jolliness and twinkles where once had been dignity and composure. Second, it gave him a team of reindeer and a sleigh to replace the white horse and wagon. Moore may well claim sole responsibility for this latter development, for the idea was borrowed from a juvenile called *The Children's Friend: A New-Year's Present, to Little Ones from Five to Twelve,* published in New York City in 1821 one year before Harriet Butler seems to have heard the poem.

> *Old Sante claus with much delight*
> *His reindeer drives this frosty night.*

It also set his arrival date as Christmas Eve rather than St. Nicholas' Eve, although as late as the Civil War Reformed Church families waited for the Visit on New Year's Eve, and some paintings inspired by the poem are entitled "The Night before New Year's." Of course, other concepts of Santa Claus ebbed slowly. In nineteenth-century engravings and drawings, the Saint comes in all sizes and shapes, appears severe as well as jovial, still wears the bishop's cross, feathers in his hat, and fur coats. Robert Weir's famous West Point painting shows him small, but not elfin, and nowhere near as jolly as modern taste would want. Even today, though most people conceive of Santa's dress and attitude in similar ways, they have no definite idea of his size. He is small enough to descend the flue, yet big enough to hold Jill on his lap.

Some people still call the Saint "Kriss Kringle" (Christ kindl, Christ-child). This, as best I can determine, stems from the popularity of two Philadelphia books of the 1840s. One, published by Thomas, Cowperthwaite, & Co., was entitled *Kriss Kringle's Book;* the other, by E. Ferrett & Co., was called *Kriss Kringle's Christmas Tree. A Holliday Present for Boys and Girls.* Except for the use of the Christ-child name, neither follows Pennsylvania Dutch, the German, concept of the gift-giver. Both stress the reindeer, fur-trimmed hat and coat, beard, and clay pipe of the Irving-Moore elf. The second book, which Henry W. Shoemaker calls the most influential Christmas book in America, even has the Christ-child hang his gifts on a *tannenbaum,* printing what are the earliest known illustrations of the Christmas tree.

It is appropriate, then, that a German, Thomas Nast, was the man who did the most to fix the concept of Santa Claus we hold today. Born in Landau, son of a Bavarian musician, Nast was brought to New York City in 1846 at the age of six. Trained from early youth to be an artist, he became a professional illustrator at fifteen, and by the time of the Civil War was one of the top commercial artists in the city, recognized (in the words of one biographer) as "a pillar" of Fletcher Harper's *Weekly,* his caricatures a powerful, political force, his mind inventing and popularizing such emblems as the Tammany Hall Tiger, the Democratic Donkey, and the GOP Elephant. When he died in 1902, he was in Guayaquil, Ecuador, where he had been appointed consul by Theodore Roosevelt.

From 1863 until 1886, Nast did a series of eagerly awaited

Christmas drawings for the *Weekly*. In them Santa Claus' year-round activities are described: his work in making toys and filling stockings, his use of a spyglass to check on young behavior, his decoration of Christmas trees, his trips about the sky in the magic sleigh. Santa Claus is even made to distribute gifts to good (that is, Union) soldiers in the Civil War, and one picture shows a Northerner on Christmas leave arriving home unexpectedly while the "jolly old elf" brings toys in the background.

Before long everyone was into the act. Professional sentimentalists like Bret Harte and Roark Bradford wrote stories about Santa Claus; poems, songs, and sermons were devoted to him and his activities. Six-packaged like so much cola, he was even hard-sold back to England, Germany, France, and Oud Amsterdam where St. Nick and Black Pete were still going their rounds. It became doctrine that children should never be disillusioned of him, and most adults never forget that "rite of passage" when voices revealed: "there *is no* Santa Claus." On September 21, 1897, the movement received its doctrine as Francis Church, an editorial writer for the New York *Sun,* replied to this letter from eight-year-old Virginia O'Hanlon:

Dear Editor:

I am 8 years old. Some of my little friends say there is no Santa Claus. Papa says "If you see it in The Sun it's so." Please tell me the truth, is there a Santa Claus?

> Virginia O'Hanlon,
> 115 West 95th Street
> New York City

Annually, Church's edict is republished, a bull for now, forever, and more.

Virginia, your little friends are *wrong*. They have been affected by the skepticism of a skeptical age. They do not *believe* except they *see*. They think that nothing can be which is not comprehensible by their little minds. All minds, Virginia, whether they be men's or children's are little. In this great universe of ours man is a mere insect, an ant, in his intellect, as compared with the boundless world about him, as measured by the intelligence capable of grasping the whole of truth and knowledge.

Yes, Virginia, there *is* a Santa Claus. He exists as certainly as love, and generosity and devotion exist, and you know that they abound and give to your life its highest beauty and joy. Alas! how dreary would be the world if there were no Santa Claus! It would be as dreary as if there were no Virginias. There would be no childlike faith, then, no poetry, no romance to make tolerable this existence. We should have no enjoyment, except in sense and sight. The Eternal light with which childhood fills the world would be extinguished.

Not believe in *Santa Claus!* You might as well not believe in fairies! You might get your papa to hire men to watch in all the chimneys on Christmas Eve to catch Santa Claus, but even if they did not see Santa Claus coming down what would that prove? Nobody sees Santa Claus, but that is no sign that there is no Santa Claus. The most real things in the world are those that neither children nor men can see. Did you ever see fairies dancing on the lawn? Of course not, but that's no proof that they are not there. Nobody can conceive or imagine all the wonders there are unseen and unseeable in the world.

You tear apart the baby's rattle and see what makes the noise inside, but there is a veil covering the unseen world which not the strongest man, nor even the united strength of all the strongest men that ever lived, could tear apart. Only faith, fancy, poetry, love, romance, can push aside that curtain and view—and picture the supernal beauty and glory beyond. Is it all real? Ah, Virginia, in all this world there is nothing else real and abiding.

No Santa Claus! Thank God he lives, and he lives forever. A thousand years from now, Virginia, nay, ten times ten thousand years from now, he will continue to make glad the heart of childhood.

Since Church's editorial, really since Livingston/Moore and Nast, there has only been one significant addition to the appearances of St. Nicholas and his retinue. This is the addition of a red-nosed reindeer as leader of the team that dashes away through the sky. Conceived originally by Robert L. May for the advertising department of Montgomery Ward, the story of Rudolph was used as a "give-away" item for the Christmas season of 1939, when about two-and-a-half-million copies of the story went out. It was not used again until 1946 when three-and-a-half-million more were distributed. In 1947, it was produced commercially and has had a steady seasonal popularity for twenty-five years now. In 1949 a song composed by Phi Bete, Johnny Marks, author of such key works as "The Ballad of Smokey the Bear" and "Holly, Jolly Christmas," was recorded by two top pluggers, Gene Autry and Bing Crosby. It swept through both the Country Western and Tin Pan Alley sides of the recording business, selling over 50 million discs, making itself familiar to nearly all Americans plus a good many Europeans and Latins as well.

The story, a variation of both the Horatio Alger success theme and the fairy-tale idea that ugly ducklings are ultimately "enswanned," tells how Rudolph, a young reindeer with a red bulb of a nose, is the butt of all the reindeer jokes. He is rejected, not allowed to play, and feels miserable. One Christmas Eve, however, the sky is foggy, and Santa (in spite of his magic) fears that he won't be able to fly. He happens upon Rudolph asleep, dreaming of Christmas presents, nose aglow in the dark. Realizing that "this is the answer," he asks Rudolph to lead the regular reindeer through the sky. Rudolph, delighted, properly leaves a note for his folks telling them where he is, and zooms off to fame and favor in reindeer circles. Santa is so delighted he commissions Rudolph to lead the sleigh every year, forever and ever.

Rudolph does seem here to stay. Stories of how pranksters painted a red-nose on a dead deer hanging from a driver's fender forcing him to deny to fearful children that he had shot Rudolph; statements from newspapers indicating that December 25 is Rudolph's, as well as Christ's, birthday; acceptance of the story by western Europeans and even Australians and South Americans; all testify to the fact that Rudolph is fast becoming a legitimate part of Christmas lore. So, if Black Pete and the handsome white horse are passing away, a red-nosed deer, appropriate to the airlanes of the twentieth century, has taken off.

And Befana–Ruprecht–Nicholas still comes to town, checking things out, rewarding the good with full socks, switching the bad. Perhaps his mission has proved overzealous. Perhaps he deserves the "sick jokes" in which he has become the lead figure: " 'Ho, ho, ho,' said Santa as he cracked the whip"; "I don't care who you are, fat man, get your reindeer off my roof"; "If you're a saint, how come you have your hand in my stocking?" Surely there's something amiss with the women's libbers who have demanded female Santa Clauses in the department stores—unconvinced, I suppose, that some "older little boy" may feel compelled to take the scarlet elf upon his knee rather than vice versa. No doubt were Jesus Christ "to preach in New York City as he preached in Galilee" he too would find this local cult "a bit too much." Nonetheless, Santa remains one of the few excursions we can still allow ourselves into the world of make-believe where right is right and wrong is wrong— period. As Gamaliel Bradford wrote, "the fairies are gone . . . the witches are gone . . . the ghosts are gone. Santa Claus alone still lingers with us. For God's sake, for Heaven's sake, let us keep him as long as we can. If God's in His Heaven, He must agree that Santa Claus is "all right for the world."

5

THE CEREMONY OF THE CAROL

ONE of the most famous legends of the Middle Ages is "The Cursed Carollers of Kölbigk." In his *Life of St. Edith,* the Flemish-born monk, Goscelin, has a pilgrim, Theodoric, tell the story. This Theodoric claims to be one of the survivors of the miracle which supposedly occurred in Saxony about 1020. "Twelve of us," he says, "gathered at the church of St. Magnus in Kolbigk on Christmas Eve." Led by a fellow named Gerluus and accompanied by two girls, Mersuind and Wibecyna, who forcibly added the priest's daughter Ava to the circle, "we joined hands and danced in the churchyard." The step was a round dance or carol, and Gerluus sang the stanzas which told how one Bovo "rode into the fair woodlands leading the fair Mersuind." Everyone echoed the refrain, "Why do we stand here? Why don't we go too?" When the priest asked the group to desist their profanations and come to services, they flippantly refused, causing such anger in the goodly father that he invoked, through the Saint Magnus, the wrath of the Lord upon them. The results were immediate, and the carolers discovered that they were unable to break their circle or stop their dancing no

97

matter how hard they tried. At one point, the priest's son, Azo, attempted to drag his sister Ava from the group, only to rip loose her arm, the stump of which did not bleed.

And so the weary dancers chanted and leaped and clapped, caroling their stanzas and the ironic refrain, "Why do we stand here?" for one whole year. "We neither ate nor drank nor slept," grieves Theodoric, "and our hair and nails did not grow. People came from all over to see us. Emperor Henry tried to have a shelter built above us, but each night the construction was mysteriously thrown down." The curse was not lifted until the following Christmas Eve, at which time the fully re-pentant carolers went into the church and slept for seventy-two hours. Nor was divine power done with its work. Ava and her troubled father soon died, while Theodoric, Gerluus, and the others were compelled to wander from land to land, each a lonely pilgrim, each with his body wracked by twitching and carol-like trembles.

This is one of the earliest references to caroling. However, carols, not only on Christmas Eve, but also on other festive dates, were common in Western Europe well before 1020. Originally pagan round dances, connected in one way or other with vegetation worship, carols became the most popular oc-casional entertainments of the Middle Ages, and medieval painting, illumination, and literature are all filled with repre-sentations of dancers in chains or circles, singing and clapping, often accompanying their steps with instruments, at all times of the year.

The Church was quite conscious of this popularity of carol-ing. For seven centuries a formidable series of denunciations and prohibitions was fired forth by Catholic authorities, warn-ing Everyman to "flee wicked and lecherous songs, dancings, and leapings," calling such affairs "slings of the Devil," showing shock that they were being performed not only in villagers' "own homes," but even "at the churches themselves." Both a council at Avignon in 1209 and one at Bâle as late as 1435 took time to issue decrees against such sinful traffic, while one Dominican compared the leader of a carol to a swineherd who, wishing all the pigs to assemble, gets one of them to squeal. Even the clergy itself was not immune to infection. In 1338, the Canons of Wells are upbraided for hurrying through the psalms so that they might hunt, fowl, fish; for "caring nothing" about the clerical state while indulging in dances and masques; for prowling the city "streets and lanes" "day and night"; as well as for leading a riotous existence "*cum cantu et tumultu.*" The nuns faltered, too. In 1442, Dame Isabel Benet of the Cistercian Priory of Catesby took a trip to Northampton to purchase supplies, but business did not fully occupy her time. She is reported to have "passed the night" with some friars "playing the lute" and dancing, an entertainment said to have been repeated the following night "in like manner."

Not only were such things a "very remnant of pagan custom," but also they caused sedition and mayhem. In 1306, for instance, a Midsummer Eve of caroling resulted in an all-night wake with much sport and, one is sure, alcoholic recreation. When a fellow named Gilbert de Foxlee tried to break up the dancing, he was stabbed in the back with a dagger, cut in the right arm with a sword, and slashed on the left leg with an axe. He died after eight weeks of infection and pain. Furthermore, a close relationship between "heathen dancing" and witchcraft had been detected. After all, the round dance with its bold leader, its carol step which went counter to the sun's motion, and its orgiastic conclusion, surely had been sanctioned by the Devil and those souls who had gained black powers through intercourse with Him.

Something had to be done, and the philosophy of "joining those you can't defeat" emerged. Francis of Assisi may not have started the wave of popular sacred song which swept across Italy and Europe in the thirteenth century, but he was certainly the major impetus in the effort to replace "riotous carols" with ones more appropriate, his· efforts, as Professor Richard Greene has pointed out, strikingly similar to those of the eighteenth-century Wesleyites and the twentieth-century Salvation Army "soldiers."

Giovanni Francesco Bernardone (St. Francis) was born in 1181 or 1182 to a wealthy textile family in Assisi. After what seems to have been a social youth, even for one of his background, he was temporarily imprisoned during the intercity feuding between Perugia and Assisi. About twenty-one, sick and unhappy, he was thus given a chance for careful self-analysis. By the time he was twenty-three, God had led him through visions and dreams which encouraged him toward conversion and penance. At twenty-five, at St. Damiano, he heard a crucifix speak, instructing him to "go repair my house, which, as you see, is falling in ruin." The result was a renunciation of his inheritance and a break with his father who neither understood nor sympathized with any such repudiation of worldly matters. Obsessed with a literal interpretation of the crucifix's order to "repair my house," Francis begged in the streets for money to restore churches and undertook the conversion of his distinguished acquaintances. By 1209, he had amassed enough followers to create an order: the Preachers of Penance (the first of three he was to initiate), and from that date his austerities are continuous; his visions and miracles frequent; his efforts to convert restless; his kindnesses to man and, particularly, beast legend. In 1224 he had stigmata on Mt. Alverna, and two years later died, blind. In 1228, he was canonized, the grave in San Francisco at Assisi concealed to remain hidden until 1818. In 1926, Pius XI styled him *alter Christus*. And in 1939, he became the Patron of Italy.

St. Francis' musical plan was to replace the "dishonest songs" of the general public with sacred revisions and inventions, attaching pious lyrics to tunes that had long been burdened with messages "worldly or worse." The result was the Italian *lauda* which was a dominant force in the popular music of the next two centuries. The greatest of all the Franciscan singers, was Jocapone da Todi, who was born in Umbria about four years after St. Francis died. Said to have been a lawyer of high birth, Jocapone was converted to a life of penance when twenty-eight after the death of his wife, the noble lady Vanna. She collapsed during a gay dance, and while attempting to tend her he discovered that she had been wearing a hair shirt under her elegant gowns. For ten years after he wandered in extreme asceticism, finally entering the Order of Friars Minor. He sang his *laudi*, exalting poverty and charity, by the roadsides under Pope Celestine V who was sympathetic to such endeavors, but got into trouble with the more staid Boniface VIII and was imprisoned. Granted amnesty in 1303 or 1304 by Pope Benedict, he died in Poor Clares Convent about 1306. Jocapone's verses, philosophical and sophisticated as they were, set a vogue, were widely sung by companies of *laudesi*, and maintained the fervor Francis had begun. His reputation was such that pieces quite foreign to his style and even some composed long after he was dead were frequently attributed to him.

What this Franciscan movement was doing to the "worldly messages" of medieval song can be illustrated in English by Friar Thomas de Hales' "A Luv Ron" ("A Love Rune) written about 1275. It seems an amorous young lady has requested that the good churchman compose her a "song of love." He obliges, but in the interests of her soul directs her to "hold fast to Christ" who is the "fairest, richest, and most steadfast" of wooers. This advice is not, however, proferred without a thorough, compassionate, and welcome set of references to great lovers of more earthly manners: fleshly men like Paris, Amadas, and Tristram; responsive women like Helen, Edayne, and Iseult.

The popular carol underwent this sort of redirection. The friars and minstrels who sang at the great halls of castle and manor also sang at the monasteries, and religious moralism was of course as regular a part of their entertainments as social moralism is of ours. Themes such as the activities of Bovo and Fair Mersuind in the woodland were asked to flourish side by side with instruction on His sorrow, His sufferings upon the Cross, His plight as a babe in a stall. Much of the "redirection" was to take place at Christmas. The twelve days, which came when the larders were still full and wintery discontent was upon the land, were the time of the major medieval feast, and the popular "carol-dancers" were as important to their success as the food itself. Thomas Gascoigne records a tale of a pious gentleman who was unable to dismiss a lewd song he had heard at Christmas and who died as a result of his guilt. In a northern romance, Sir Cleges recalls how he wasted his entire estate on a Christmas feast and how well he rewarded the minstrels who came and performed. The enemies of the human race join in a "Christmas Song" in the 1475 morality play called *Mankind*. And carols are a feature of the mid-winter festivities going on at the Court of Arthur as *Sir Gawain and the Green Knight* begins. Moreover, Christmas was a target quite appropriate for Franciscan zeal. St. Francis himself had taken a particular interest in the Nativity and the little Christ, possibly lured by its stress on humility and poverty. Traditionally, he is supposed to have instituted the custom of the crèche, and, as we have seen, his name is often associated with the ox and the ass, two "dumb creatures" of the many he loved and was kind to. Christmas, with its penchant for caroling, demanded, and got, full attention.

The result, at least where the carol is concerned, was an "uneasy peace" in the long power struggle between pagan ritual and Catholic belief. The old songs lived: processionals which signal the commencement of pagan feasting—

> *The Boare is dead,*
> *Loe, heare is his head,*
> > *What man could haue done more*
> *Then his head of to strike,*
> *Meleager like,*
> > *And bringe it as I doe before?*
>
> *He liuinge spoyled*
> *Where good men toyled,*
> > *Which made kinde Ceres sorrye;*
> *But now, dead and drawne,*
> *Is very good brawne,*
> > *And wee haue brought it for yu.*
>
> *Then sett downe ye Swineyard,*
> *The foe to ye Vineyard,*
> > *Lett Bacchus crowne his fall,*
> *Lett this Boares-head and mustard*
> *Stand for Pigg, Goose, and Custard,*
> > *And so yu are welcome all.*

—stanzas which mark out the ancient rivalry between the holly male and the ivy female,

> *Nay, Ivy, nay, hyt shal not be iwys,*
> *Let Holy hafe the mastery, as the maner ys.*

The "new" songs abounded: hymns which are filled with adulation,

> *Hayl, Mary, ful of grace,*
> *Moder in virginite.*

or frank religious rejoicing,

> *"Nowell, nowell!"*
> *This is the salutacion off the aungell Gabriell.*

Soon the two were mingling, their symbolisms confused:

> *The borys hede that we bryng here*
> *Betokeneth a Prince withowte pere*
> *Ye born this day to bye us dere;*
> *Nowell, nowelle!*

One of the most famous carols even makes "ivy" the symbol of the Virgin Mother and notes, nearly glibly, that Mary bore Christ on Christmas morn "as the holly bears the prickle as sharp as any thorn." It's no wonder that in traditional dancing the holly is able to symbolize the triumphant Crusader and the ivy the conquered Moor or that the handy ivy is able to replace the palm in Palm Sunday processions. Such mixtures never bothered medieval Christians anyhow. They often mingled mirth (or "cheerfulness" as they called it) with devotion. For, as Professor Greene has pointed out, the grace doesn't make a meal into a religious service, nor in any way impair "the merriment and good fellowship of the table."

By Tudor times, the form and subject matter of the carol was ranging about as far as license could take it. There were ballad-like pieces such as "The Cherry-Tree Carol" and "Stephen and Herod"; lullabies to the Babe of Bethlehem as he sleeps in the manger; macaronic pieces with their English stanzas and Latin burdens; cumulative lyrics like "The Boar's Head," question-and-answer songs like "The Seven Virgins." Perhaps the most common of the types to develop was the "call to the neighbors" to awake and visit the crèche. In such carols, the Holy Family is conceived in terms of the singers themselves: Mary suffering in labor, hovering over a baby who shivers on the straw; Joseph weary, scared, bumbling and grumbling about; the neighbors overflowing with good will, pitching in, bringing appropriate gifts such as warm milk in a pan, chunks of meat, coverlets of lambskin, pipes, horns, and toys for the child, even boughs to soften his bed. The American Negro spiritual telling how "po' little Jesus" had no cradle, had no bed, and commenting "Wasn't that a pity, wasn't that a shame" catches the spirit precisely.

And by Tudor times the carol had irrevocably associated itself with Christmas, not only in the "demi-Paradise," but also on the Continent where similar songs (the French *noël*, the German *weihnachtslied*, the Greek *kálanta* were flourishing. Not that the carol was never to grace a mid-summer revel or a spring parade again,

> Mery hyt ys in May morning,
> Mery wayys for to gone;

not that children weren't to trace the old steps in their playground games or their parents to dance the familiar patterns at frolics and country hoedowns; but that Christmas was to become the main time for caroling and the phrase "a Christmas carol" was to begin to suggest to all but the scholar much the same thing as the word "carol" alone. Thus the *Encyclopaedia Britannica* can describe the carol as "a hymn of praise, especially such as is sung at Christmas in the open air"; *The Standard Dictionary of Folklore, Mythology, and Legend* will call carols "a traditional song type in English, originally unrestricted in subject matter ... but for centuries associated with the Christian celebration of Christmas ..."; and *The Oxford Book of*

Carols is able to state that "Carols are songs with a religious impulse that are simple, hilarious, popular, and modern"—and to "anyone who knows" all three definitions make good sense.

It must be obvious by now that ritual is the hardest thing in the world to stamp out. Officials can pound their fists, stamp their feet, forbid, declare, enforce, but if people are in the habit of doing certain things at certain times of the year they are going to find a way to continue—regardless! By the time the Puritans came on the scene in England, western Europe, and the Colonies, Christmas and its side-play was deeply established ritual and it was going to take a lot more than "blue law logic" to eliminate it. Much has been made of the Puritan ban of Christmas, stage shows, and other profanations, and the average citizen thinks of his New England forebears as sitting gruffly indoors for "twelve days" each year like so many grizzlies. Actually, the Puritans didn't object to the celebration of the Tide of Christ so long as that celebration was in the proper spirit. What they did oppose was the Tide of Yule with its caroling, gaming, mimic performances, and intimations of orgy. Such confusion they deemed a prostitution of the Christ Mass spirit, and when they realized Christ and Yule had become inseparably intertwined they cast out the package. For they were "purifiers," and their business was first to rid the Anglican Church and then the State of unnecessary and distracting embellishments—not only of vestments, services, and offices left over from Rome, but also of sometime pagan indulgences. Where they gained control of the government, in England from 1649–1660, in New England from 1620 to about 1680, they pounded their fists, forbade, and enforced. Revels were made illegal, the public theaters were closed, and "merry" Christmas was banned, which does not mean that mummers, minstrels, and dancers did not continue their activities in remote areas or under cover, that plays weren't performed at private homes or in abridged versions at country fairs, or that Christmas rites weren't acted out sometimes under the very noses of the presbytery itself. The famous passage from Pilgrim Governor William Bradford's *Log Book* shows not only how difficult it is to get people to "behave," but throws a good bit of light on how a sensible Purifier really felt.

Having excused some of a "new company" of men from work on Christmas because the men "saide yt went against their consciences to work on yt day," the Governor goes off with "ye rest" to the chores at hand. When the group comes back for a noontime break, they are aghast to find "ye rest" in "ye streets at play openly, some pitching ye barr, and some at stooleball and such like sports." Bradford at once takes away their "implements" and tells them it is "against his conscience that they should play and others work." He concludes, wryly, "If they made ye keeping of it matter of devotion, let them kepe their houses, but ther should be no gameing or revelling in ye streets. Since which time nothing hath been attempted that way, at least openly." Bradford's conclusion is, incidentally, quite in the spirit of Martin Luther, who, enemy of "wicked papistrie" though he were, has been depicted at least once playing the lute midst his family on Christmas Eve, beside a lighted Christmas tree, before a table loaded with fruit and bread and a tankard of nut-brown ale.

Nevertheless, men like Increase and Cotton Mather were to press a more Geneva-oriented approach. In 1659, the General Court of Massachusetts forbade, at the penalty of five shillings per offense, the observation of "any such day as Christmas or the like, either by forbearing of labour, feasting, or any such way," while in Connecticut the law prohibited the reading of Common Prayer, the keeping of Christmas or saints' days, the making of minced pies, playing at cards, or performing on any instrument of music, except the drum, trumpet, and Jew's harp. And looking at matters through Calvinistic eyes, we can hardly fault these guardians of order as we recall the description of the Canterbury riot in Chapter I or the passage in Philip Stubbs' *The Anatomie of Abuses* where he tells how Christmas Day revelers march on a church with pipes playing, drums thundering, bells jingling. The intruders are dressed as hobby horses and "other monsters," and they skirmish among the crowd with "such confused noise that no man can hear his own voice" though "the minister bee at prayer or preaching." What's worse, the "foolish people" in the congregation look, stare, laugh, and "feer," even mounting the pews and forms to see better, as the mummers enter, whirl up and down the aisles, go out again, parade round and round the building, ending the profanation by setting up banquet tables in the churchyard.

But no historian in his right mind thinks that the prohibitions were any more successful than those which today prohibit the smoking of marijuana. By 1681, when Puritanism had been eclipsed in England and when immigration into Massachusetts had diluted Puritan control, the former law had become so impossible to implement that it was repealed. Normally cheery Samuel Sewall, growling in his *Diary* during the 1680's and '90's, blesses God that he doesn't have to observe the Christmas occasion and rejoices that the shops are open, but it is obvious even to his narrow eyes that "some, somehow, observe the day." What was happening in Massachusetts was happening even faster elsewhere, and by the end of the century Christmas was swelling toward full tide once more.

Still, there is no doubt that Puritan objections to the Christmas revels restrained the flow of carol tradition. For nearly one generation in England and for a good bit longer than that in the New England colonies, the old carols were preserved only in outlandish memory, on broadsides produced by underground printers, or through manuscripts such as the *Commonplace Book* of Richard Hill, grocer's apprentice and literary pack rat.

City people, polite people, had little access to such things, and it takes no longer to forget a Christmas ditty in the seventeenth century than it does to forget a "golden oldie" in the twentieth.

Seventeenth- and eighteenth-century religion favored their own types of popular religious music anyhow: psalm-singing whereby the minister entoned a phrase which the congregation echoed back to him as individual fancy dictated: country fuging, a variant of the round; "shape-note" reading, in which the notes of the "sol, fa" scale are distinguished by their shape as well as their place on the staff. But these styles were not polite styles. Polite religious singing, like all music of the *beau monde*, came to be dominated by classical traditions, especially by the efforts of Handel and Haydn. And it is classical tradition that is most responsible for those hymns of comfort and joy which come immediately to the city mind when the word "carol" is mentioned.

To survey the musty books of the "Christmas carols" which have found their way onto library shelves over the last 275 years is to arrange a rendezvous with history, for most anyone with "an ear for a phrase" was liable "to try his hand" at celebrating the delights of the groaning board or the glories of a "new-born king." Many of the *essais* want genius.

> *All you that to feasting and mirth are inclin'd,*
> *Come here is good news for to pleasure your mind,*
> *Old Christmas is come for to keep open house,*
> *He scorns to be guilty of starving a mouse;*
> *Then come, boys, and welcome for to diet the chief,*
> *Plum-pudding, goose, capon, minc'd pies, and roast-beef.*

But good, bad, or most likely mediocre, certain pieces have become standards, favorites whose vintage is such they lie beyond literary reproofing. While on the list of authors stands many a name revered in another context. There is Nahum Tate, best known for his happy rewriting of Shakespaere's *King Lear*, a revision which replaced the Bard's masterpiece on the boards for nearly 150 years. As early as 1715, Tate wrote "While Shepherds Watched Their Flocks by Night" setting his words to the "Christmas Melody" from Handel's opera *Siroe*. There is "spiritual Quixote" Charles Wesley, uncle of Methodism, who adapted Felix Mendelssohn's *Festegang* music to carry the phrase "Hark, the Herald Angels Sing," a phrase which really ought to be "Hark, How All the Welkin Rings." There is Isaac Watts, whose "O, God Our Help in Ages Past" and "Am I a Soldier of the Cross?" are among our most famous hymns, and who wrote "Joy to the World" in 1748, though it wasn't for 124 years that the present setting by Lowell Mason was developed out of tunes in Handel's *Messiah*. There is Henry Wadsworth Longfellow, progenitor of such national idols as Paul Revere, Hiawatha, and Evangeline, who wrote a poem which begins "I heard the bells on Christmas Day" in 1863 after his son had been seriously wounded in the Civil War, and which is now sung to an English tune called "Waltham."

The "background notes" to the songs have their own trivial fascinations, filled as they are with "dear legends" telling how "this carol came to be composed" or how "that carol arrived at its present form." Browsing, one can learn that Martin Luther did not really write "Away in a Manger," so often called "Luther's Cradle Hymn." But rather that the words were written by some long-forgotten Pennsylvania Dutchman who was inspired by a Luther hymn, *"Von Himmel kam der Engel Schar"* with its opening line *"Ein Kindlein zart, das liegt dort in der Krippen."* This poem was printed in Philadelphia in 1885 and nearly a half-hundred settings have been composed for it since. One of the most popular is by James R. Murray, who innocently ascribed the text to Luther in 1887. We find out that the origin of *"Adeste Fidelis"* still baffles scholars. The original Latin poem is often ascribed to "the Seraphic Doctor," Bonaventure, the thirteenth-century Franciscan saint, but few seriously believe he wrote it. The manuscript containing text and tune dates from the 1700's and is signed by John Francis Wade, an English music dealer working in Douai, France, a fact which complicates life for those who would have Marcus Antonius de Fonseca, nineteenth-century chapelmaster to the King of Portugal, as the composer. We read that the "first American carol" was written by Jesuit martyr and saint, Jean de Brébeuf who worked among the Hurons from 1626 until he was captured and tortured to death by the Iroquois in 1649 or 1650. Father de Brébeuf had written a Christmas hymn entitled "Jesus is Born" in the Huron language using a French folksong as melody. The song survived until it was recorded by Father Étienne de Villeneuve at a reservation near Quebec. When Villeneuve died, the carol turned up in his papers and in the nineteenth century was translated into French. Recently it has had some circulation in the United States and Canada as rewritten and reset by J. E. Middleton and Edith Thomas.

The legend of good King Wenceslas is there. Wenceslas was a tenth-century duke, not king, in Bohemia. He is recalled by Christians because he helped spread the faith in what is now Czechoslovakia, was martyred, and attained sainthood. A miracle which occurred on a bitter cold December 26, the Feast of Stephen, forms the basis of the "carol"—a poem set to the melody of a sixteenth-century spring canticle by nineteenth-century John M. Neale. It tells how the "king" and his page were tramping through the "crisp and even" snow to fetch a poor man to a feast he had no reason to think he would attend. As the page begins to freeze, he is instructed to step into Wenceslas' footprints which give off sufficient heat to make him comfortable. The event may well have been a miracle, for it is often stated "in the notes" as having occurred in 935, although the "good king" was murdered as he was entering a church in Stará Boleslav in 929. The murderer was his younger brother, named Boleslav, who coveted power and, noticeably upset over the recent birth of a direct heir, was urged to action by political conspirators.

These legends, like all legends, tend to follow patterns. One of the most common formulas is illustrated by the "origin stories," which center on the need for a new carol, the pressure of time, and the fact that the "inspired song" lies neglected for years after its initial performance. "*Stille Nacht, Heilige Nacht*" was written near Salzburg in 1818. It seems that Joseph Mohr, the parish priest of the small town of Oberndorf, was told on Christmas Eve that the organ, which had broken down a few days before, would not be ready for Midnight Mass. As this meant that the music for High Mass could not be performed, Father Mohr decided to assuage his flock with a new Christmas song. He sat down and penned "Silent Night," recalling he said the sight of an ailing mother and her baby whom he had visited during his rounds that day. When the text was finished, he took it to his friend Franz Gruber, who was organist in nearby Arnsdorf. Gruber, inspired, composed the melody almost at once and that night the first performance of the song was given to the accompaniment of a guitar. The hymn was forgotten almost at once, lying hidden among the choir manuscripts for years. Finally, it was rediscovered and popularized by a family of singers, the Rainers, who toured Europe and America in the 1830's and '40's much in the fashion of the Trapp family of more recent times. Now it is perhaps the best loved of all Christmas anthems sung across the world. Oberndorf has seen fit to raise a monument to Father Mohr and his Arnsdorf friend Franz Gruber.

Strikingly similar is the famous tale of how Phillips Brooks composed "O Little Town of Bethlehem." Brooks, it seems, was talking with his organist in Holy Trinity Church, Philadelphia, during Advent in 1868. He was anxious to have a fresh carol for his Christmas Day Sunday School service. In his mind was a poem he had jotted into a notebook in the fields outside Bethlehem as he stood deeply moved on Christmas Eve three years earlier. The organist, Lewis Redner, under great pressure from seasonal obligations, came through, inspired, writing the melody "out of hand." The hymn was used in 1868, then forgotten. It wasn't until twenty years had passed that it was rediscovered, printed in a local paper, and swept to its present vogue.

As this flurry of metropolitan music-making was going on, the old carols, the true carols, were pretty well ignored. In *Singing Family of the Cumberlands* Jean Ritchie describes her childhood in Viper, Kentucky, forty-to-fifty years ago and talks about the typical rural Christmases. It is noteworthy that in this backwoods community the carols that the family sings are the very ones known in the American cities of the 1920's and '30's: "Silent Night," "Away in a Manger," "Noel" (as she calls it), "Good Christian Men Rejoice," "The Holly and the Ivy," "I Saw Three Ships Come Sailing In," and "Star in the East." Obviously among the Kentucky mountaineers the true carol had disappeared completely, probably before the ancestors came over. Jean's grandmother stresses that "when she was a little girl, nobody in the country round really celebrated Christmas":

It was more of a religious time then, and it fell on the sixth of January. Old Christmas we call it now. And then we didn't make a great to-do. . . .

When Christmas did return, it was the songs from the cities, not the "forgotten ones," that came into use.

But recently, as the study of antiquity and folkways has become fashionable, many of the old carols have been revived, resuscitated after more years of neglect than those suffered by *"Stille Nacht"* or "O Little Town of Bethlehem." Enthusiastically gleaned from old broadsides pasted on cottage walls, copied from reprints of commonplace books where they have lain hidden among recipes and sentimental verse, harvested from the scattered country people, who were never instructed to discard them, they have once more crowded their way into the Christmas repertoire, creating a mosaic that mingles city hymns of merry-rested gentlemen, midnights clear, and Oriental kings with medieval macaronics, pagan ivy, four colley birds, *El Niño Jesus,* po' little Jesus, and a Virgin Mother whose name is pronounced "Wary" because the Huron language has no "M."

And sometimes the modern mosaic seems so democratic that it lacks any sort of distinction as it groups Irving Berlin, Jacopone da Todi, Phillips Brooks, and George Frederick Handel side by side. Not that the everyday has ever been foreign to caroling, but that somehow there is cacaphony in hearing a sixteenth-century spring canticle which bears the tale of a tenth-century Bohemian miracle either before or after "Elvis the Pelvis" regrets the "blue, blue Christmas" he must suffer "without you." Like a latter-day Samuel Sewall, one can close the chapter by recording that as Brenda Lee "rocks" annually "around the Christmas tree" in that circular path so long associated with the old caroler a certain something does get lost in her shuffle.

6

SEEKING JESUS

No one who has studied medieval literature forgets the *quem quaeritis* trope just as no one who has taken second-year Latin forgets *"Gallia est omnis divisa in partes tres."* In its simplest form, *quem quaeritis* is an interchange between the angel guarding the tomb from which Christ has arisen and the Three Marys who come to anoint the body with spices—the scene of Matthew XXVIII, Luke XXIV, Mark XVI.

GUARDIAN ANGEL: Whom do you seek in the tomb, Christian women?
THREE WOMEN *with spices:* Jesus of Nazareth Who was crucified, celestial one.
GUARDIAN ANGEL: He is not here; He has arisen as was foretold. Go announce that He has arisen out of the tomb.

This "wart upon the Mass," as one merry medievalist termed it, was first added as an Introit to the Easter Sacrament in the tenth century, probably in Switzerland. Once introduced, it spread rapidly, not only to other lands, but to the matins and to other Masses at other times of the calendar. The little repartee

115

is the fountainhead out of which our western European drama flows.

That a part of the Easter Mass is the source of a Nile which eventually includes Shakespeare, Shaw, and even Hollywood is not surprising. After all Easter was the central rite of medieval worship, a gripping commemoration of the most critical moment in The Life. As it developed from mere symbolic celebration into an actual repetition of the initial sacrifice, it lent itself to pomp, circumstance, and dramatic embellishment. So the bishop and his processional might enter the church to thuds from a staff, fan the thick air with palm fronds, and chant impres- sively at critical points in the service. So feet might be bathed, torches flare or be extinguished at proper moments, stories of the Passion be intoned by narrators selected for their voices (tenors for the words of the evangelists, basses for the words of Christ). Because the laity could not comprehend Latin, trans- lations and bits of the vernacular were introduced. Comedy and mimicry of local figures were fostered. Appropriate ani- mals were brought in, their brayings and indiscretions adding to the fun. Pretty nuns or even prettier town girls might play the feminine roles. And dialogue, like the *quem quaeritis*, flourished.

St. Ethelwold of Winchester gives the scenario for the Third Nocturn at matins on Easter morning about 976.

As the third lesson is being chanted, let four of the brothers put on vestments. Let one of them, wearing an alb, enter as if to take part in the service, approach the sepulchre without fuss, and sit there quietly with a palm in his hand. While the third respond is being chanted, let the remaining three follow after, and let all of them, wearing copes, carrying thuribles with incense in their hands, approach the sepulchre with the delicate steps of those who seek something. These actions are done in imitation of the angel sitting on the monument and of the women with spices who come to

anoint the body of Jesus. Thus, when he who is sitting sees the three
approach him like people who are lost and who are seeking something, let him begin to sing in a soft voice of medium pitch: *Quem
quaeritis*. When he has sung it through, let the three reply in unison,
Ihesu Nazerenum. To this he replies, *Non est hic, surrexit sicut
praedixerat. Ite, nuntiate quia surrexit a mortuis*. At the word of
this bidding, let the three turn to the choir and say *Allelulia!
resurrexit Dominus!* This spoken, let the one sitting there say the
anthem *Venite et videte locum*, as if calling them back. Saying this,
let him rise and lift the veil and show them the place bare of the
cross with only the clothes in which the cloth was wrapped laid
there. When they have seen this, let them put down in the sepulchre
the thuribles which they carry and take up the cloth, holding it in
the face of the clergy as if to show that the Lord has risen and is no
longer wrapped in it. Then let them sing the anthem *Surrexit
Dominus de sepulchro* and place the cloth upon the altar. When
the anthem is done, let the prior begin the hymn *Te Deum laud-
amus*, sharing their joy at the triumph of our King in that having
conquered death He rose again. And this begun, let all the bells
chime out together.

The setting of such a performance was simple, requiring few
properties or costumes beyond what vestments and ornaments
the church normally supplied. The Marys had their heads
veiled and wore surplices, copes, chasubles, dalmatics, albs, and
the like. Mary Magdalene might be in red, the others in white.
The angel or perhaps angels sitting inside the sepulchre or at
the door had white vestments, their heads crowned. Sometimes
they also wore wings, and they held lights or palms or corn to
symbolize the Resurrection. The apostles were in ordinary
priestly robes, John holding a palm, Peter the keys. One or
the other might carry a cross or even a spade. All the "actors"
were priests, nuns, and choir boys, except in unusual cases.

Over the years, the performances were "envigorated." Stock
characters and scenes developed. The Marys purchased the
spices from a crafty merchant, the pall was lifted discovering

the empty tomb, the grave-garments were cast off, Peter and John raced to the sepulchre, Mary Magdalene encountered the gardener.

Naturally, such excitements couldn't be confined to Easter alone. Almost at once, the twelve days of Christmas developed its own group of tropes and dramatic vanities. In fact, an early Christmas trope which begins *Quem quaeritis in praesepe, pastores, dicite?* appears in the eleventh century. A crèche, watched over by an image of the Virgin Mother, was set behind the altar where a choir boy dressed as an angel sang his nowells to five vicars who came forward as if shepherds. There they were met by two priests who posed the inevitable question: "whom do you seek?" The tabloid, which came to be known as the *Officium Pastorum,* usually concluded with a hymn of adoration.

The Easter offices have long since vanished from most of the Catholic world, but variations of this Christmas scene live on. Soon Joseph, ox, and ass join the Mother in her vigil over the swaddled child. Vignettes depict the rise of the Eastern Star and detail the gifts of the Magi. Playlets tell Rachel's tale. Character sketches show Herod ranting, raving, hurling books about in his rage to destroy the infants of Bethlehem. Possibly because of the obsession of St. Francis and the Franciscans with the crèche, the Christmas offices have survived the removal of the tropes from the services, their development outside the church walls in vernacular texts, their performance by parish groups, guilds, and wandering troups. They replace the Resurrection as the featured scene in those miracle or mystery plays which recount the *cursor mundi,* the history of the world as told by the Bible and Saints' legends, enduring association with legends as peripheral as those about Veronica and Tiberius or Joseph of Arimathaea.

But the performance of the mysteries and miracles did not

occur in December. A festival for entire districts, they were given in all-day cycles usually at Corpus Christi in late May or early June when the weather was more suitable for open-air acting. The plays were either presented on stands placed in a circle along which the crowd moved or, more commonly, were given in procession on wagons drawn by horses or lowly apprentices. The wagons served as rolling stages and the performances were repeated at designated street corners or before shops of merchants who had paid for the privilege in significant towns like Chester, Norwich, Wakefield, or Newcastle-upon-Tyne. These "pageants" might have three decks—Heaven on high, Earth in the middle, Hell and the dressing-rooms below. From a hole in Hell belched smoke and from time to time the Devil emerged without rehearsal, waving his pitchfork and soliciting jeers and boos. A sturdy spectator could stand still and see twenty-five to fifty plays and a good bit of affiliated entertainment in a day that really went from dawn to dusk.

At the height of this tradition, the sponsors were the trade guilds, guided by the town corporations, who selected parts of "the story of the world" in keeping with their particular commerce: the story of the ark for the shipwrights or carpenters; of the Last Supper for the bakers; of the Magi for the goldsmiths; and, of course, of the Nativity for the sheep-herds. The preparation was careful. Lavish sums were spent on props and costumes, like gloves for God and robes for Herod; actors were well rewarded with food, goods, and approbation usually on a scale proportionate to the dignity of their role, God being worth thrice what Noah was. Biblical personalities were given local twists. Mrs. Noah had a shrewish temper and a woman's traditionally cold feet; the Devil was a medieval Simon Legree; the Virgin Mother was a lovely, sweet thing; the shepherds griped about low wages and frost-bitten hands. The plots were biblical, but the settings, the dialogue, and the cast was quite contemporary. The tone was at least as much "fun" as religion.

Two or three days before the festivities, heralds would go through the town and the surrounding areas announcing the plays and even describing them scene by scene. When Corpus Christi arrived, the town throbbed. Work ceased. The equivalents of Cokes, hot dogs, and mustard rolls were hawked. "The cymbals clanged, the drums banged, and the horns went root-tee-toot." If one thinks of the Pasadena Tournament of the Roses today, then modifies it to fit a smaller and more naive world, he understands. For in its medieval way the whole matter was big business, big enough so that some towns even built fixed stages in churchyards or large fields to accommodate hundreds of spectators and so that some guilds sent their performers to act in outland communities.

Of all the miracle plays produced during this more than 500 year era, the play once acted at Wakefield in the reign of Henry VI (1422–1461) and now called *The Second Shepherd's Play* is surely the best. It is easy to forget that it is a Christmas "office" with an ancestry that runs directly back to the *Officium Pastorum*. The reason we forget is that the play has two parts: one long and comic, made from an ancestor of this Ozark folktale—

There was a man stole a pig from his neighbor. The neighbor had his suspicions, so him and the sheriff made a little visit to the man's home. They knocked and got no answer, so they damn near pounded the door down. Finally, the man opened the door and said, "For God's sake take it easy. We've got a sick baby in here." The sheriff says we're sorry, but we came to get the pig you stole from your neighbor. The man says, "Don't talk to me about no pigs when my baby's got small-pox."

As soon as he heard the word "small-pox," the neighbor high-tailed it out of there for fear he'd catch the disease. But the sheriff said he'd had small-pox, and that it was his duty to search "these here premises." He looked all around, but couldn't find the pig. Just as he was leaving he said, "Let me see that baby, I'll tell you whether he really has small-pox or not." The man said "No one's going to look at my sick baby. Sheriffs are for catching thieves and all that, but they don't pull no covers off sick children." This made the sheriff mad, and they began to argue and shove each other. While they were scuffling, they bumped the cradle and the "baby" began to wiggle about and go "oink, oink." So the sheriff jumped over and pulled the covers off and there was a pig lying in the cradle. It weren't no baby at all. However, when the sheriff turned around to arrest the man, he had run out of the house. I don't know if they ever caught him or not.

—the other brief and solemn, made from Luke, I, II, 8:

And there were in the same country shepherds abiding in the field, keeping watch over their flocks by night.

The balance so established indicates how easily entertainment can outstrip religion in audience appeal, in this case the sugar-coating just about eliminating room for the pill.

The anonymous author, whom scholarship has fatuously labeled "The Wakefield Master," opens his Christmas "office" "in fields" where "certain poor shepherds" keep watch. One, the rascal Mak, steals a sheep while his companions sleep. Drawing a magic circle so that the sleepers will remain put, he lugs the sheep home to his sharp-tongued wife Jill (Gill) Without time to kill it and dress it as mutton, they wrap it in baby's clothes and place it in a cradle. Later the shepherds awaken and noting the lost sheep begin to look for it. The search leads them to Mak's cottage where the trick deceives them largely because of Jill's reputation for steady fecundity. They leave. Unfortunately, one of them recalls that they have forgotten to bring the "new baby" presents. So they return and ask to give him sixpence and to kiss him. As they pull back the coverlet they are startled by the long snout and ugly features, Mak and Jill attempt to brazen things out by claiming the "baby" has been "forespoken" and switched by an elf for a fairy changeling. But the jig is soon up, and Mak, exposed, is tossed in a blanket for his greed. Satisfied now, the shepherds go back to sleep. Before long they are reawakened by an angel who sings *"Gloria in excelsis"* and directs them to Bethlehem to see another new-born babe. The play ends as Mary tells them of God's power and Christ's birth. They bid "farewell" to the "lady so fair to behold with thy child on thy knee" and depart singing.

The wagon on which this play was once acted has been re-constructed as thirty feet long. At one end probably stood Mak's house. The fields with the shepherds were probably in the center. At the opposite end was Bethlehem with the stable and a crèche. It is a simple set for simple souls, yet *The Second Shepherd's Play* is much more sophisticated than the average medieval miracle. Its pace is fast, its lines are witty, its characters and situations are "the best." Mak and Jill are incorrigibles, lovers of life and the excitement of crime. Mak, suspected of the theft, points to the "child" in the cradle and swears "to God" that "this be the fyrst male that I shall ete this day." Jill picks up the lead, insisting if she is guilty she will eat "this child" that lies in the cradle. The shepherds gripe over high taxes, the idleness of the rich landowners, the shrewish dispositions of their wives. One warns young bachelors to be "well war of wedying," pointing out that once you are in you are in for good. Yet all have the capacity for awe. They are amazed by the angel, and they select their gifts for the Christ-child (a bob of cherries, a bird, a tennis ball) with naivete and adoration. "It holds, as 'twere, the mirror up to nature."

The Second Shepherd's Play is seldom revived today. But given a good translation, it would make excellent Christmas entertainment, its comedy, its characters, its situations arresting to anyone who loves to watch "what fools mortals be." Like *Volpone, The Beggar's Opera,* or *Charley's Aunt,* it is simply "good theater," its "can't miss" label none the less for being fifty-five decades old. The English cycles gave way to other forms of drama, to moralities, interludes, and Elizabethan masterpieces, well before the days of Jamestown and Plymouth Rock. Even without the Puritans, the English church plays had no chance to cross the ocean. Yet, thanks to the polyglot nature of our land, dramas quite similar to *The Second Shepherd's Play* can still be seen within the United States and performed in a tradition that runs pure back to the medieval world. These are the Spanish *coloquios* of the Mexican southwest.

In Spain, the Christmas offices went under the name *autos del nacimiento.* They flourished in the fifteenth and sixteenth centuries when such writers as Juan del Encina, Gil Vincente, and Lucas Fernández lent them genius much in the fashion of the Wakefield Master. For instance, in Encina's *Egloga de las grandes lluvias* of 1498 four shepherds are lolling about a fire discussing the heavy rains and floods in the region. They have started to gamble when an angel appears with the news that *El Salvador* has been born. One of the shepherds hears the word as *El Saludador* (The Greeter) and confusion results. Eventually this *juego de palabras* gets straightened away, and the shepherds decide to set out for Bethlehem to honor the Christ with gifts. They present Him with a little dog, a linnet, a small kid, some cheese, honey, a few spoons, and a flagon of blood. The excitement ends with the singing of some *villancicos,* popular Christmas songs.

In fact, the overall situation in Spain, as in western Europe at large, was much like that in England, and a typical spring saw the *autos* being performed during Corpus Christi in the streets of the towns. *Carros,* portable stages, were used, and it was not unusual for the cast, rather than the crowd, to move

from stage to stage as the scenes changed. Church interest in
the performance was intense, and it was natural to bring this
form of festive edification to Mexico after the Conquest, three-
fourths of a century before Jamestown, twenty-five years before Shakespeare's birth. As the friars went about their business
of traveling the wilderness, building missions, converting "los
indios," the *autos* proved worthy tools. In 1539, Fray Toribio
Motolinia, a contemporary of Hernando Cortes, described a
production of *Adán y Eva* in the town square at Tlaxcala.
Live animals and birds were used to help simulate the Garden;
the actors were Indians who spoke their native Nahuatl; and
the spectators were so moved by the expulsion of the couple
from Paradise that most wept. Motolinia also explains that the
Indians were instructed how to set up a *nacimiento* or crèche
and how they brought gifts to *El Niño* as he lay in his
"manger."

The Mexican Indians of the sixteenth century were scarcely
more sophisticated than the medieval peasants. The plays that
the friars selected to enliven their Christianity also had to be
simple in characterization and action with large interludes of
coarse comedy. The lines were obviously and frequently rhymed
to facilitate memorization and were best received when bom-
bastic. The plots were the stock-in-trade *cursor mundi* stories:
Adam and Eve; Cain and Abel; the flight of San José and
family into Egypt; the search for *Las posadas,* lodgings, in Bethlehem; the Nativity; the tale of *Los reyes magos,* the wise men;
the account of *El Niño perdido,* the boy Jesus' visit to the
Temple in Jerusalem; the Passion. But it was not unusual for
miracles that had occurred in the New World, like the appearance of the Virgin at Guadalupe, or dance-dramas, like the
conflict of *christianos* with *moros* to be mimed.

The term *Los pastores* (the shepherds) has become a catchall
covering such matters. It honors the focal event: the *Nacimi-*

ento which is still reenacted, not at Corpus Christi, but during the warm Christmas-tide from the Mexican states of Zacatecas and Jalisco northward to Colorado and mid-California. In 1940, one scholar recorded thirteen performances of the Nativity story from the state of New Mexico alone. The plot is the familiar one: the pilgrimage of the shepherds to Bethlehem to see the crèche. The Devil always tries, but fails, to disrupt the journey, and there is the climactic scene where the humble, peasant gifts are offered to the new-born babe. Though the stress is much more heavily on the religious side of the story, with more frequent interludes of carols and dance, the similarity between these contemporary *pastorelas* and *The Second Shepherd's Play* is arresting.

The *pastorelas* are usually given in the afternoon or early evening of December 24, though some communities hold extended runs during the whole Christmas season. Today, a favorite place for production is the patio or corral of a *mesón*, an inn, though the atrium of the local church will do. The audience consists of most of the people in town, who bring their own chairs from their homes. The actors are fellow townsmen who have rehearsed for several weeks, learning their lines under the tutelage of a director who has access to a *cuarderno* (copybook) preserved in the town hall or church library. Many actors play the same roles year after year, often developing a following and eventually passing their mantle to a successor in the true folk way.

In 1891, Captain John Bourke, medal of honor winner in the Civil War, Indian fighter, and amateur ethnologist, was stationed in the Rio Grande Valley. Fascinated by the life of the natives, he left a hoard of notes and handsomely illustrated diaries, the originals of which are presently squirreled away in the archives of the United States Military Academy at West Point. In 1893, he published a description of a *pastorela* that had been performed in Rio Grande City, Texas, while he was there. It begins,

As the holy season of Advent approaches, one cannot fail to notice among the inhabitants of the Mexican ranches and towns of the Lower Rio Grande, Texas, a degree of bustle and unwonted activity, particularly about the hour of sunset, which indicates that the normal placidity or apathy of life has been seriously disturbed, and that some grand "funccion," more important than wedding, funeral, christening, baile, or even "marromas" (tight-rope walkers) or "tetires" (puppet-show), is in process of incubation.

Inquiry will elicit the reply: "Pues, son los pastores, no mas,"— (Why, it's nothing but the Shepherds!), while a more persistent investigation will be rewarded with the information that the "pastores" are having an "ensayo," or rehearsal of their dramatic representation of the "Nacimiento," or birth of the Saviour in Bethlehem. . . .

The *locus* of the play is supposed to be Palestine, and the *dramatis personae* include, besides the Holy Mother and Babe,—whose presence, however, in our days is suggested rather than revealed, as a présibi, or manger, is generally erected, before which the actors stand,—a Chorus of Shepherds and Shepherdesses, a Head Shepherd, Michael the Archangel, Lucifer and several of his Imps, and an aged "Ermitaño," or Hermit, whose life has been passed in devout contemplation, and who now, bent with age and hoary of beard, admonishes and advises the ignorant herders who resort to him for spiritual consolation.

There are several rather ludicrous incongruities which may be recognized without giving offence to the pious fervor of the actors and actresses, who become intensely wrought up in their parts as the plot unfolds. The Hermit carries, attached to his waist, a rosary made of wooden spools, and bears in his right hand a large crucifix, although the Saviour has not yet been born and his Passion is all yet to be undergone. In every case that I saw or heard of, the rosary was made of these large wooden spools.

Whenever it could be conveniently done, Lucifer was dressed in the uniform of a cavalry officer, but time is working changes, and at this writing his Satanic Majesty enacts his rôle in raiment not so pronouncedly martial.

For weeks beforehand the actors selected meet under the superintendence of the Head Shepherd (in the present case an intelligent cobbler), and listen attentively and patiently while he reads, line by line and word by word, the part of each. Very few of them can read or write, and none of them in a manner betokening extensive practice; the dependence for success, therefore, is almost wholly upon eye, ear, and memory, and the rehearsals are repeated again and again, until every man, woman, and child can recite the lines almost mechanically.

These roles are stock roles, designed not only to follow the biblical details of the shepherd story, but also to exploit themes that are certain to elicit laughter from simple-minded people. There is, of course, the central struggle between Lucifer, who regrets the birth of man's Saviour, and the agent of the Lord, Archangel Michael, who will lead the shepherds to the manger. Lucifer, dressed in black with a long red train, horns and feathers topping his head, is accompanied by an assistant, Asmodeo. He hovers about the shepherds waiting for one to feel slighted so that he may be dissuaded from the journey. Sometimes Lucifer rants and raves, sometimes he begs and wheedles; usually he pauses long enough to retell the story of his revolt against Awe. Asmodeo, dressed like his Master, but with a blue train, is named after a Hebrew spirit devoted to breaking up marriages. Today, his evil has lost any such grandeur of purpose, and he is a fatuous, ineffectual buffoon. Michael, white-robed, with wings and a sword to vanquish Lucifer, is so exalted he can have little personality. Most often the role is given to a thirteen- or fourteen-year-old girl. As Bourke remarks, "Both Michael and Lucifer rant a little too much to satisfy critical taste, but allowance must be made that the event they contemplate is the crucial epoch in the life of mankind, and both are speaking to influence suffrages in their favor."

The fun of the play, as in the Wakefield masterpiece, comes from the shepherds and their friends: from Bato, Bartolo, Gila, Blanche Flor, the Hermit, the farmer, and the Indian. These characters are designed to capitalize on the belly laughter inherent in extreme laziness, gluttony, frivolous old age, and rural stupidity. Like Mak, Gila's husband, Bato, offers the principle comic relief. Bato is a boor, who thinks of nothing but food and rest, even to the point of sleeping while he is eating. At the crèche, he invariably dozes off during the presentation of the gifts and may take a nap in his joy at hearing of Jesus' birth. The name Bato, now a Mexican colloquialism roughly equivalent to the English "guy" once actually was the slang term for "thick, lazy hick." Sometimes this role is given to Gila's father, Bartolo. Sometimes both are present. Like the other shepherds they wear colored shirts, short cloaks, and straw hats decorated with mirrors, beads, and bright cloth. Gila does not usually have a major role, at least not one as vigorous as that of the Wakefield Jill. With her are a group of shepherdesses, one usually called Blanche Flor. They are dressed in the same sort of shirts and short cloaks as the men, although their garments are pink and virginal white. So casually defined are their personalities that sometimes all of them go under the one name, "Gilas." Much more interesting is the Hermit, who is 200 or so years old, yet indulges in vigorous singing and dancing. He wears a long monk's robe with a hood. Around his neck is a rosary of squash stems, and he carries a cross. However, his most important property is a whip, which he swings at members of the audience who move too near him. A typical scene has the Hermit offering Gila a few herbs for dinner, being rebuked for such a miserable contribution, and then sulking so that Lucifer sees a chance to tempt him. There is also a *Ranchero* or small farmer who knows little of town ways. Wearing country clothes, he rolls his own cigarettes in the country way, rides a horse, and has a lariat, saddle-bags, and other equipment. The *Ranchero* may sit down in the presence of the Virgin Mother or ask Joseph to repair his pots and pans. Usually, the Hermit ends up whipping him for his boorishness. Finally, there is an Indian, unsophisticated, childlike, poorly garbed, speaking with a marked accent, which is a source of continual humor to both the audience and the shepherds.

"The first rehearsal which I witnessed," says Bourke,

lasted over three hours, and all the others nearly the same time, yet both actors and audience maintained a stolid and dogged attention beyond all praise.

The music is inferior and the singing execrable, because the voices of the women and men of the Lower Rio Grande are generally too attenuated and stridulous to be pleasing; nevertheless there are occasional snatches of harmony which dwell agreeably in memory.

Unlike the theatrical and acrobatic representations, there are no fixed charges for admission to the "Pastores;" those who have money are expected to pay, and those who have none are made welcome without it. But, much after the manner of the Christmas carols of Old England, the "Pastores" will gladly go from house to house of the more wealthy, enacting their parts with all due fervor, and expecting in return a largess of hospitality and a small pittance in money.

The church of late years has set its face against the appearance of the "Pastores" within the walls of sacred edifices, but they are looked upon as innocent and harmless, and free scope given them within their present circumscribed limits.

As the proof of the pudding is in the eating, it may be well to let my readers form for themselves an idea of the language and plot.

The libretto, containing between eight and ten thousand words, of which passages are given below, was written out for me by Francisco Collazo, the Head Shepherd.

The shepherds have just learned from the Archangel Michael the glad tidings of great joy, and have burst out in paeans of praise and gratitude:—

In the Gate of Bethlehem
There is great light,
For there has been born the Messiah
Who is to set us at liberty.

En et portal de Belen
Hay muy grande claridad,
Porque allá nació el Mécias
Y el nos pondrá en libertad.

And so on through seven verses more, none of significance, excepting the one in which Gila, the Shepherdess, is commanded by the Chief Shepherd to get ready plenty of "tamales" for the subsistance of the shepherds during their journey to Bethlehem. . . .

Lucifer, called Luzbel in the libretto, now rushes upon the scene and indulges in frenzied soliloquy: "Driven out of heaven by the sword of Michael on account of proud ambition and infamous crime, I boasted of my fault, for the earth was still mine. But what is this I hear? These songs of gladness,—these victorious chants of seraphim? What is this I hear of the Star newly seen in Arabia?" Then he bethinks himself that the fulfilment of time is at hand, the seventy weeks of Daniel have expired, and the prophecies of Ezekiel are accomplished. In Bethlehem he learns that in a manger oxen and asses have kept warm with their breath a little babe whom his fears tell him only too plainly is the Incarnate Word.

There is a very considerable amount of this soliloquy, and it is evident to the most careless listener that Luzbel, or Lucifer, is not at all pleased with the prospect opening before him. . . .

Luzbel is, of course, powerless to dissuade the shepherds. Michael sees to that. To make a "long sermon short,"

The Infernal One is soon disposed of, and the shepherds find themselves in front of the manger of Bethlehem.

There is a great increase in the number of hymns and prayers of adoration, each of the shepherds chanting a hymn and reciting a prayer while he deposits his gifts.

Parrado expresses his surprise that the Holy Infant is so small, and hopes he may soon grow big enough to play with his (Parrado's) nephew, "Andrecito."

The gifts are varied, but very cheap, and seem to consist mainly of flowers, bed linen, clothing, playthings, honey, food, and silver, which last is said to have been made by a "platero" (silversmith) from Mexico, a detail which enables us to fix the date of the composition as later than A.D. 1520....

The final songs include one of the alphabet, in which each letter is credited with certain qualities, but exactly what all this means it would be hard to say....

It is not hard, however, to say exactly what the "Christmas offices" mean and have meant as a group. Their Christian message is consistently loud and clear. Far vaguer and more baffling is that body of drama we now turn toward—miming, also called mumming, masqueing, guising, and "geese dancing."

7

"GEESE DANCING"

DURING the centuries when the clerics and friars were active in drama, neither the folk nor the courtiers were idle. In England, as in the rest of Europe and the Colonies, derivatives of pagan ritual persevered under the general title of "mumming," a word used to describe a group of sometimes approved, sometimes banned activities ranging from morris dancing, wassailing, even parading to boxing, caroling, court reveling, and the enactment of ritualistic plays. Central to mumming are the twin ideas of playing a part (miming) and of wearing masks (guising or geese-dancing). Normally mummers are male. With their followers, they move about a community demanding gifts for their entertainments, have the right to enter homes and areas that might otherwise be barred, and are able to dispense with dignity and politeness. On January 3, 1528, when Henry VIII burst into Cardinal Wolsey's supper party as one of a group of sixteen masked revelers, he was doing it under seasonal, as well as regal, license. The spirit in which mumming is carried on is reflected in a proclamation once issued by the Sheriff of York who announced, surely with resignation, that "all manner of whores and thieves, dice-players, carders, and all other unthrifty folke, be welcome to the towne, whether they come late or early, at the reverence of the high feast of *Youle,* till the twelve dayes be passed."

In the courts, colleges, on huge estates, and in some towns, mumming was actually under the supervision of a "Lord of Misrule" who was annually elected to oversee the excitement. This Lord of Misrule, also called the Abbot of Unreason and the Christmas Prince, is of considerable antiquity, the position undoubtedly having a heritage parallel to that of the Church's Archbishop or Pope of Fools. As William Hone says in his *Ancient Mysteries,* mock pontiffs were elected to serve at Twelfth Night, at New Year's, or on some other appropriate mid-winter day and seem "to have been one of the recognized revels of the Christmas season." The Archbishop of Fools was permitted a "proper suite of ecclesiastics" and one of his

. . . ridiculous ceremonies was to shave the Precentor of Fools upon a stage erected before the church in the presence of the jeering "vulgar populace."

They were most attired in the ridiculous dresses of pantomime players and buffoons, and so habited entered the church, and performed the ceremony accompanied by crowds of followers representing monsters or so disguised as to excite fear or laughter. During this mockery of a divine service they sang indecent songs in the choir, ate rich puddings on the corner of the altar, played at dice upon it during the celebration of a mass, incensed it with smoke from old burnt shoes, and ran leaping all over the church. The Bishop or Pope of Fools performed the service and gave benediction, dressed in pontifical robes. When it was concluded he was seated in an open carriage and drawn about the town followed by his train, who in place of carnival confetti threw filth from a cart upon the people who crowded to see the procession.

These "December liberties," as they were called, were always held at Christmas time or near it, but were not confined to one particular day, and seem to have lasted through the chief part of January.

When the ceremony took place on St. Stephen's Day they said as part of the Mass a burlesque composition called the Fool's Prose.

The Lord of Misrule acted in similar fashion. In Norfolk in the fifteenth century,

John Hadman, a wealthy citizen, made disport with his neighbours and friends, and was crowned King of Christmas. He rode in state through the city, dressed forth in silks and tinsel, and preceded by twelve persons habited as the twelve months of the year. After King Christmas followed Lent, clothed in white garments trimmed with herring skins, on horseback, the horse being decorated with trappings of oyster-shells, being indicative that sadness and a holy time should follow Christmas revelling. In this way they rode through the city, accompanied by numbers in various grotesque dresses, making disport and merriment; some clothed in armour; others, dressed as devils, chased the people, and sorely affrighted the women and children; others wearing skin dresses, and counterfeiting bears, wolves, lions, and other animals, and endeavouring to imitate the animals they represented, in roaring and raving, alarming the cowardly and appalling the stoutest hearts.

There is little doubt that these and related festivities have an immemorial history which weaves back to winter rites designed to purify the houses and fields at the New Year and to confound the spirits by disguise, mocking the sacred, switching sex roles, noise, and unusual dress or behavior. The God Comus oversaw such things in ancient Greece, and the old Roman Empire knew them too, as an account by Caesarius of Arles, concerning the January Kalends in sixth-century Gaul, testifies:

On those days the heathen, reversing the order of all things, dress themselves up in indecent deformities.... These miserable men, and what is worse, some who have been baptized, put on counterfeit forms and monstrous faces, at which one should rather be ashamed and sad. For what reasonable man would believe that any men in their senses would by making a stag turn themselves into the appearance of animals? Some are clothed in the hides of cattle; others put on the heads of beasts, rejoicing and exulting that they have so transformed themselves into the shapes of animals that they no longer appear to be men.... How vile, further, it is that those who have been born men are clothed in women's dresses, and by the vilest change effeminate their manly strength by taking on the forms of girls, blushing not to clothe their warlike arms in women's garments; they have bearded faces, and yet they wish to appear women....

But mumming is not exclusively a mid-winter activity, and many brooks feed its mainstream over the centuries. British misrule celebrations have mingled their ancient symbolisms with such seeming irrelevancies as Hock-Tuesday dramas recalling the defeat of the Danes by the English in 1002; May Day rites honoring the Sherwood Forest poacher Robin Hood; and summer sword dances echoing crusades of Christian soldiers against Devilish, dark-skinned Moors.

These sword dances are noteworthy, not only because they are so similar to the Christmas plays, but because the dancers indulge in guisings quite like those of the misrule festivities. Sir Walter Scott saw one on August 7, 1814.

At Scalloway my curiosity was gratified by an account of the sword-dance, now almost lost, but still practiced in the Island of Papa.... There are eight performers, seven of whom represent the Seven Champions of Christendom, who enter one by one with their swords drawn, and are presented to the eighth personage, who is not named. Some rude couplets are spoken (in *English,* not *Norse*), containing a sort of panegyric upon each champion as he is presented. They then dance a sort of cotillion going through a number of evolutions with their swords.

The sword dance is an old ceremony in its own right, going far back into Anglo-Saxon history, its symbolic miming not at all well explained by scholars. Obviously, it is thought that the Christian champions, normally the following saints: George of England, James of Spain, Denis of France, David of Wales, Patrick of Ireland, Anthony of Italy, and Andrew of Scotland are really modern developments of earlier pagan heroes, and it is fashionable to see them as fertility forces involved in the winter-spring business. In some of the dances the leader wears a fox-skin to cover his head with the tail hanging in the rear. Called a "tommy," he is usually accompanied by a "bessy," a man dressed as a woman. Other characters like True Blue, Jolly Dog, or Little Foxey, as well as tailors, vintners, sailors, and the like abound. The action consists of dances, advances and withdrawals to music, and the performance of sword drills. The rhyme at the end of the Shetland "play" is typical:

> *Mars does rule; he bends his brows:*
> *He makes us all aghast.*
> *After the few hours that we stay here*
> *Venus will rule at last.*
> *Farewell, farewell, brave gentles all,*
> *That herein do remain!*
> *I wish you health and happiness*
> *Till we return again.*

The St. George plays and mummers' plays, which are definitely Christmas activities, are so closely related to the sword dances that the main characters are just about interchangeable. However, in the plays, there is something approaching a plot, with a character (or series of characters) slain and revived. In the St. George variants, a Turkish Knight usually slays George, who is resurrected by a comic "doctor." All such plays include music and dancing, frequently the sword dance itself, and feature assorted "tommies" and "bessies," in addition to the very important Dragon, Father Christmas, and Beelzebub. At the conclusion, Beelzebub or a clown makes the rounds with a frying pan begging money from the crowd.

Like other misrule rites the mummers' and St. George plays have attracted their share of bagatelle over the years. When seen through uninitiated eyes, they can appear outright preposterous:

IN PARIS, MEN ARE MEN, GIRLS ARE GIRLS; BUT IN ENGLAND —

By Robert Musel

LONDON, Dec. 23. — (UP) — The pantomime or silly season is here again and producers are busy trying to make a boy out of beautiful Jacqueline De Bief—which shows you just how silly it is.

Pantomime is something that happens only in Britain around Christmas time. Its roots are somewhere in the dim past and tourists often wonder why the whole thing wasn't nipped in the bud right then. But the British love it.

Miss De Bief is the undulating Frenchwoman who won the world's skating championship a couple of years ago. She signed to play the lead in "Aladdin on Ice" and showed up for her first rehearsal.

"You play a boy," she was informed.

Miss De Bief looked down at herself.

"I cannot play a boy," she said, "obviously."

"That's all right," said the producer. "You play a boy but we want you to look like a girl. The more legs etcetera, the better."

Miss De Bief did not quite understand this. In Paris men are men and women are women and no one has yet been able to think of a better arrangement.

"That man," said the producer, "plays the mother. He's called a 'Dame'."

"Would it not be better to have the mother played by a woman?"

"This is pantomime," snapped the informant. "Now you fall in love with this beautiful girl."

"Played by a man, I assume."

"Of course not. She is played by a girl."

"But the love scenes?"

"No kissing."

At this point Miss De Bief said "crazee" and collapsed into French.

But she had only heard part of the story. Although it is called "pantomime" which means dumb show, these extravaganzas are filled with noise, music, singing, shouting, dialogue. Although they are supposed to be for children, this dialogue is often adult enough to bring blushes to manly cheeks.

The fact that the dame is played by a man usually results in a bit of horseplay involving his upstairs stuffing. The kiddies just laugh and laugh.

Most pantomimes incorporate popular songs of the day. Thus Jack clasps Jill to his bosom and sings "Wait for Mary." No one minds.

For that matter, the "cast" of the mummer's play Marie Campbell discovered in a Kentucky mountain community of the 1930's might well confuse the actors themselves:

THE CAST

THE PRESENTER.   Not in costume.

FATHER CHRISTMAS.   Santa Claus suit borrowed from the school. Holly in his beard. Carried a frying pan and a dead rabbit.

DAME DOROTHY.   A man dressed in bright colored woman's clothes. Veil made of an old window curtain served as a mask. Red paper pinned inside the front of her dress was displayed later as blood.

OLD BET.   A man dressed as an old woman. Apron, bonnet and shawl. Mistletoe on bonnet.

THE BESSIE. A man dressed as a woman with a cow's tail fastened on. Grotesque mask of brown paper with horns sticking up. Holly on the horns. Carried two cowbells strung across his hips.

LITTLE DEVIL DOUBT. A boy with his face blackened. A hump on his back. Gay red paper streamers tied around his arms and neck. Holly on his hat.

PICKLE HERRING. A man wearing a woman's "bedgown" under a man's overcoat. Carried an inflated pig's bladder colored like a balloon. A dunce cap with gay streamers served as a mask. Many floating red paper streamers.

DOCTOR GOOD. A man wearing a long-tailed coat, spectacles, and a very high top hat. Face painted very red. No other mask. Holly on his hat. Carried a doctor's bag.

CHORUS. Eight high school boys wearing the white smocks of the home economics class. Paper bags over their heads as masks. Holly wreaths around their necks.

Certainly St. George, who Oriental legend tells us was ripped into ten parts before being picked up and restored to life by the Archangel Michael, makes an appropriate combination death-revival hero and Christian champion by means of whom the old ways can be continued. April 23, his day, was celebrated in the Middle Ages by processions, contests, and festivities of a municipal, that is not fully ecclesiastical, nature. Because he was a guild patron, some towns gave their miracle plays on April 23 instead of Corpus Christi. Because the Order of the Garter was under his protection, there was usually a feast at court like the famous one given at Windsor in 1416 for Henry V and Emperor Sigismund of Germany. One can be sure dancing, singing, and other sorts of mumming abounded.

I have never read a satisfactory explanation of why the St. George plays are now associated with Christmas when "his day" is in the spring. It seems the performances just cropped up at this major holiday of the year after they had become well-es-

tablished in medieval life and after the masses had acquired
an insatiable taste for them. Perhaps it was because they were
considered a form of mumming, and mumming was so integral
to Christmas. Whatever, they did eventually fix themselves to
the Twelve Days, although here and there communities have
insisted on performing them in the spring or at totally "inap-
propriate" times of the year.

In 1865, one W. Kelly printed a St. George Play from the
manuscripts of the Borough of Leicester in a version that was
"performed in some of the villages near Lutterworth, at Christmas 1863." It is quite characteristic of the Christmas mumming
dramas, if somewhat abbreviated.

THE CHRISTMAS MUMMERS' PLAY

Dramatis Personae

1. CAPTAIN SLASHER, *in military costume, with sword and pistol.*
2. KING OF ENGLAND, *in robes, wearing the crown.*
3. PRINCE GEORGE, *King's Son, in robes, and sword by his side.*
4. TURKISH CHAMPION, *in military attire, with sword and pistol.*
5. A NOBLE DOCTOR.
6. BEELZEBUB.
7. A CLOWN.

Enter CAPTAIN SLASHER: I beg your pardon for being so bold,
    I enter your house, the weather's so cold,
    Room, a room! brave gallants, give us room to sport;
    For in this house we do resort,—
    Resort, resort, for many a day;
    Step in, the King of England,
    And boldly clear the way.
Enter KING OF ENGLAND: I am the King of England, that boldly
    does appear;
    I come to seek my only son—my only son is here.

Exit PRINCE GEORGE: I am Prince George, a worthy knight;
    I'll spend my blood for England's right.
    England's right I will maintain;
    I'll fight for old England once again.
Enter TURKISH KNIGHT: I am the Turkish Champion;
    From Turkey's land I come.
    I come to fight the King of England
    And all his noble men.
CAPTAIN SLASHER: In comes Captain Slasher,
    Captain Slasher is my name;
    With sword and pistol by my side,
    I hope to win the game.
KING OF ENGLAND: I am the King of England,
    As you may plainly see,
    These are my soldiers standing by me;
    They stand by me your life to end,
    On them doth my life depend.
PRINCE GEORGE: I am Prince George, the Champion bold,
    And with my sword I won three crowns of gold;
    I slew the fiery dragon and brought him to the slaughter,
    And won the King of Egypt's only daughter.
TURKISH CHAMPION: As I was going by St. Francis' School,
    I heard a lady cry 'A fool, a fool!'
    'A fool,' was every word,
    'That man's a fool,
    Who wears a wooden sword.'
PRINCE GEORGE: A wooden sword, you dirty dog!
    My sword is made of the best of metal free.
    If you would like to taste of it,
    I'll give it unto thee.
    Stand off, stand off, you dirty dog!
    Or by my sword you'll die.
    I'll cut you down the middle,
    And make your blood to fly.
    (They fight; Prince George falls, mortally wounded.)
Enter KING OF ENGLAND: Oh, horrible! terrible! what hast thou
    done?
    Thou hast ruin'd me, ruin'd me,

By killing of my only son!
Oh, is there ever a noble doctor to be found,
To cure this English champion
Of his deep and deadly wound?

Enter NOBLE DOCTOR: Oh yes, there is a noble doctor to be found,
To cure this English champion
Of his deep and deadly wound.

KING OF ENGLAND: And pray what is your practice?

NOBLE DOCTOR: I boast not of my practice, neither do I study in the
practice of physic.

KING OF ENGLAND: What can you cure?

NOBLE DOCTOR: All sorts of diseases,
Whatever you pleases:
I can cure the itch, the pitch,
The phthisic, the palsy and the gout;
And if the devil's in the man,
I can fetch him out.
My wisdom lies in my wig,
I torture not my patients with exactions,
Such as pills, boluses, solutions, and embrocations;
But by the word of command
I can make this mighty prince to stand.

KING: What is your fee?

DOCTOR: Ten pounds is true.

KING: Proceed, Noble Doctor;
You shall have your due.

DOCTOR: Arise, arise! most noble prince, arise,
And no more dormant lay;
And with thy sword
Make all thy foes obey.   (*The Prince arises.*)

PRINCE GEORGE: My head is made of iron,
My body is made of steel,
My legs are made of crooked bones
To force you all to yield.

Enter BEELZEBUB: In comes I, old Beelzebub,
Over my shoulder I carry my club,
And in my hand a frying-pan,
Pleased to get all the money I can.

Enter CLOWN: In come I, who's never been yet,
    With my great head and little wit:
    My head is great, my wit is small,
.   I'll do my best to please you all.
Song (all join): And now we are done and must be gone,
    No longer will we stay here;
    But if you please, before we go,
    We'll taste your Christmas beer.   (*Exeunt omnes.*)

It is a variant of this Leicester play that Thomas Hardy made famous in Chapters 4 and 5 of Book II of *The Return of the Native,* a novel which was read by just about every American high school and college student in the decades before the Second World War. It made Vye and Yeobright household names and caused James Thurber to comment that the only thing he had learned from his English classes at Ohio State was that he would like a date with Eustacia Vye.

In the novel, Eustacia is aroused by Clym Yeobright because of her boredom, because he has frequented "that rookery of pomp and vanity" Paris, and because of his voice—in this order. It is Christmas-tide. When Charley, one of the local mummers, comes to seek permission to use the Vye's fuel-house to rehearse the St. George Play, Eustacia sees her chance to "scout" a hero "who might possibly have the power to deliver her soul from a most deadly oppression." She strikes a bargain with Charley, exchanging the chance to secretly take his part in the play for a half an hour of "holding your hand in mine." Charley's role is that of the Turkish Knight, one which the quick-minded Eustacia memorizes almost at once. The bargain is carried out, Charley bringing the trappings over to the Vye's house and claiming the payment.

"Here are the things," he whispered, placing them upon the threshold. "And now, Miss Eustacia—"

"The payment. It is quite ready. I am as good as my word."

She leant against the door-post, and gave him her hand. Charley took it in both his own with a tenderness beyond description, unless it was like that of a child holding a captured sparrow.

"Why, there's a glove on it!" he said in a deprecating way.

"I have been walking," she observed.

"But, miss!"

There are, of course, elaborate "behind the scenes preparations," carried on by the sweethearts and wives of the mummers.

... Without the co-operation of sisters and sweethearts the dresses were likely to be a failure; but on the other hand, this class of assistance was not without its drawbacks. The girls could never be brought to respect tradition in designing and decorating the armour; they insisted on attaching loops and bows of silk and velvet in any situation pleasing to their taste. Gorget, gusset, basinet, cuirass, gauntlet, sleeve, all alike in the view of these feminine eyes were practicable spaces whereon to sew scraps of fluttering colour.

Thus the young ladies vie with one another, adding "brilliant silk scallops," ribbons, and bows or rosettes in a competition "not to be outdone."

The result was that in the end the Valiant Soldier, of the Christian army, was distinguished by no peculiarity of accoutrement from the Turkish Knight; and what was worse, on a casual view Saint George himself might be mistaken for his deadly enemy, the Saracen. The guisers themselves, though inwardly regretting this confusion of persons, could not afford to offend those by whose assistance they so largely profited, and the innovations were allowed to stand.

In Chapter 5, the play is presented at the conclusion of a dance the Yeobrights have given for the "plain neighbors and work people." Even though her fellow players guess her to be

"Miss Vye," a revelation she counters with "You may think what you like . . . But honorable lads will not tell tales upon a lady," Eustacia gets through her role without being discovered, dying, "sinking by degrees until quite overcome," and finding leisure "to observe the scene around and to search for the form that had drawn her hither."

Hardy clearly knew a good lot about St. George drama, and some of his personal recollections of the mummers are "there for the reading" in William Archer's book, *Real Conversations*:

MR. HARDY. ... Then, again, the Christmas Mummers flourished well into my recollection—indeed, they have not so long died out.

W. A. I can remember a sort of mummers in Scotland whom we called "guisers"; but they were simply boys wearing masks and begging for half-pence.

MR. HARDY. Oh, our mummers hereabouts gave a regular performance—*The Play of St. George* it was called. It contained quite a number of traditional characters: the Valiant Soldier, the Turkish Knight, St. George himself, the Saracen, Father Christmas, the Fair Sabra, and so on. Rude as it was, the thing used to impress me very much—I can clearly recall the odd sort of thrill it would give. The performers used to carry a long staff in one hand and a wooden sword in the other, and pace monotonously round, intoning their parts to one note, and punctuating them by nicking the sword against the staff—something like this:—
"Here come I, the Valiant Soldier (*nick*), Slasher is my name (*nick*)."

W. A. The pacing and rhythmic sing-song suggest kinship with the Chinese acting I have seen in San Francisco and New York. And what was the action of the play?

MR. HARDY. I really don't know, except that it ended in a series of mortal combats in which all the characters but St. George were killed. And then the curious thing was that they were invariably brought to life again. A personage was introduced for the purpose—the Doctor of Physic, wearing a cloak and a broad-brimmed beaver.

W. A. How many actors would there be in a company?

MR. HARDY. Twelve to fifteen, I should think. Sometimes a large village would furnish forth two sets of mummers. They would go to the farmhouses round, between Christmas and Twelfth Night, doing some four or five performances each evening, and getting ale and money at every house. Sometimes the mummers of one village would encroach on the traditional "sphere of influence" of another village, and then there would be a battle in good earnest.

W. A. Did women take part in the performances?

MR. HARDY. I think not—the fair Sabra was always played by a boy. But the character was often omitted.

W. A. And when did the mumming go out?

MR. HARDY. It went on in some neighbourhoods till 1880, or thereabouts. I have heard of a parson here and there trying to revive it; but of course that isn't at all the same thing—the spontaneity is gone.

The comment is elaborated on in the novel:—

For mummers and mumming Eustacia had the greatest contempt. The mummers themselves were not afflicted with any such feeling for their art, though at the same time they were not enthusiastic. A traditional pastime is to be distinguished from a mere revival in no more striking feature than in this, that while in the revival all is excitement and fervour, the survival is carried on with a stolidity and absence of stir which sets one wondering why a thing that is done so perfunctorily should be kept up at all. Like Balaam and other unwilling prophets, the agents seem moved by an inner compulsion to say and do their allotted parts whether they will or no. This unweeting manner of performance is the true ring by which, in this refurbishing age, a fossilized survival may be known from a spurious reproduction.

Obviously in Boston, the drama which remained vigorous in Leicester until the end of the nineteenth century survived as a fossil, becoming little more than a silly sidelight to a trick as well as treat revel. "I forget," writes Samuel Breck in his *Recollections . . . with Passages from His Note-Books (1771– 1862)*:

on what holiday it was that the Anticks, another exploded remnant of colonial manners, used to perambulate the town. They have ceased to do it now, but I remember them as late as 1782. They were a set of the lowest blackguards, who, disguised in filthy clothes and ofttimes with masked faces, went from house to house in large companies; and, *bon gré, mal gré*, obtruding themselves everywhere, particularly into the rooms that were occupied by parties of ladies and gentlemen, would demean themselves with great insolence. I have seen them at my father's, when his assembled friends were at cards, take possession of a table, seat themselves on rich furniture, and proceed to handle the cards, to the great annoyance of the company. The only way to get rid of them was to give them money, and listen patiently to a foolish dialogue between two or more of them. One of them would cry out, 'Ladies and gentlemen sitting by the fire, put your hands in your pockets and give us our desire.' When this was done, and they had received some money, a kind of acting took place. One fellow was knocked down and lay sprawling on the carpet, while another bellowed out,

> "See, there he lies,
> But ere he dies
> A doctor must be had.

He calls for a doctor, who soon appears, and enacts the part so well that the wounded man revives. In this way they would continue for half an hour, and it happened not unfrequently that the house would be filled by another gang when these had departed. There was no refusing admittance. Custom had licensed these vagabonds to enter even by force any place they chose. What should we say to such intruders now? Our manners would not brook such usage a moment.

And this in spite of the fact that Christmas was not being celebrated in Boston in those days and in the face of a 1753 law
banning all "mummers and pageants in the streets."

There are many such "fossils." Two Irish-Canadian ladies
named Boville are able to recall their youth in the Belfast of
the 1860's.

On Christmas Eve . . . , young boys gather together and dress
themselves up, supposedly in imitation of cavaliers, by pulling
their shirts out over their trousers, and wearing on their heads large
hats made from folded newspaper, with paper fringes and a large
paper tassel on top. The boys go from house to house, bursting
noisily in at the door, and in turn each one steps out and recites
his verse. They are given money, apples, nuts, etc., by the people
whose houses they enter.

FIRST BOY
     Here comes I, Beelzebub,
     And over my shoulder I carry my club,
     And in my hand a dripping-pan,
     I think myself a jolly old man.
SECOND BOY (carrying broom over his shoulder).
     Here comes I, wee devil Doubt.
     If you don't give me money, I'll sweep you all out.
     For it's money I want, and money I crave.
     If you don't give me money, I'll sweep you all to your grave.
THIRD BOY (representing Oliver Cromwell).
     Here comes I, long Copper Nose,
     I fought the jolly Dutchmen, as you may well suppose.
     I fought the jolly Dutchmen until their hearts did quake.

. . . .

While in Fife, Scotland, today,

Men and women, boys and girls, dressed themselves in strange
costumes, and blackened their faces, or otherwise disguised them,
and went off to village and farmhouses, sang songs, and danced to

the banter and amusement of the onlookers. It was rare fun not to be known. . . . Then the ability and cleverness of those who detected the "guisers" were something to boast about. Sometimes a strong youth would seize a damsel, and keep her in his clutches until he was sure of her identity, but he might get into trouble by the walking-sticks of the males under whose protection she was placed.

And in Dorsetshire,

The Bull, shaggy head with horns complete, shaggy coat, and eyes of glass, was wont to appear, uninvited, at any Christmas festivity. None knew where he might or might not appear. He was given the freedom of every house and allowed to penetrate into any room, escorted by his keeper. The whole company would flee before his formidable horns, the more so as towards the end of the evening, neither the Bull nor his keeper could be certified as strictly sober.

For such is the way of ritual as man proceeds in stubborn rote with what his forebears left him: forgetful of meanings; hindered by unsympathetic times; even, as Hardy says, without any deep feelings.

Nonetheless, ritual, made vulnerable by half-remembered meanings and weakened symbolism, inevitably must fall into foreign hands and absorb matter as irrelevant as Robin Hood or St. George to a fertility rite. When Booker T. Washington watched the Negroes during those "Anxious Days and Sleepless Nights" at Tuskegee, he saw them in slavish imitation of the White Christmas.

The coming of Christmas, that first year of our residence in Alabama, gave us an opportunity to get a farther insight into the real life of the people. The first thing that reminded us that Christmas had arrived was the "foreday" visits of scores of children rapping at our doors, asking for "Chris'mus gifts! Chris'mus gifts!" Between the hours of two o'clock and five o'clock in the morning I presume that we must have had a half-hundred such calls. This custom prevails throughout this portion of the South to-day.

During the days of slavery it was a custom quite generally observed throughout all the Southern states to give the coloured people a week of holiday at Christmas, or to allow the holiday to continue as long as the "yule log" lasted. The male members of the race, and often the female members, were expected to get drunk. We found that for a whole week the coloured people in and around Tuskegee dropped work the day before Christmas, and that it was difficult to get any one to perform any service from the time they stopped work until after the New Year. Persons who at other times did not use strong drink thought it quite the proper thing to indulge in it rather freely during the Christmas week. There was a widespread hilarity, and a free use of guns, pistols, and gunpowder generally. The sacredness of the season seemed to have been almost wholly lost sight of.

But the John Kuners (John Connus) of Reconstruction days in Wilmington, North Carolina, had managed to fuse African ways with British ways in a Creole parade that may have been imitative when it began in the Bahamas, but which had developed into something quite unique by the time it strayed into the American South.

They were dressed in "tatters", strips of cloth of gay colors sewn to their usual garments and producing an effect of exotic grotesquerie. All were men, but a few wore the clothes and acted the parts of women. The leaders of the band and the women actors frequently wore masks known as kuner faces. These kuner faces were painted upon something like buckram and presented features most remarkably distorted, enormous noses, widely grinning mouths, horns and beards, fierce and terrifying to behold. The leader carried a raw-hide whip with which he prevented interference from urchins in the streets; so he was greatly feared by small boys. The band of Kuners, consisting of ten to twenty negroes, drew up in the street before the assembled group of white people and began their show. The leader stood out in front of his group and sang the verses of his song, the others joining in the refrain while they rattled their bones, made of beef ribs, and made noises upon the cows' horns, triangles, and jew's-harps. The songs proceeded to tunes not remarkable for their melody but of pronounced rhythm. The solo voice sang the first and third lines, the effect being much like that of the familiar negro working or camp meeting songs.

SOLO:	Young *gal* go ROUND de corner!
CHORUS IN HARMONY:	My true love gone DOWN de lane!
SOLO:	Wet on de grass where de djew been poured.
CHORUS:	HEY, me lady, go DOWN de road;
	Go DOWN de road; go DOWN de road!
	My true love gone DOWN de lane.

Another song describes the arrest of a negro known as Beau Bill whose offence was the conduct of a dance-hall.

Old Beau Bill was a fine old man,
A riggin' and a roggin' in the world so long;
But now his days have come to pass,
And we're bound to break up Beau Bill's class.

Refrain

So sit still ladies and don't take a chill
While the captain of the guard house ties Beau Bill.

After the song, one of the dancers, performing "chicken in the bread tray" or "cutting the pigeonwing", would approach the spectators with his hat held out. Having collected large copper pennies, the Kuners danced off down the street to the next house where they were welcomed by another group of expectant children. On rare occasions, when the collection was not equal to their expectations, they sang as they went away,

"Run, Jinnie, run! I'm gwine away,
Gwine away, to come no mo'.

Dis am de po' house.
Glory habbilulum!"

Dancing, rattling bones, and shouting,

"Hah! Low! Here we go!
Hah! Low! Here we go!
Hah! Low! Kuners comin' ".

The whirling mob turns the corner and is lost to view until another Christmas brings the horrible features, songs and antics again
into the streets.

In America today, the most vigorous survival of "geese dancing" is the costly, carefully rehearsed Philadelphia Mummers'
Parade. Part circus, part minstrel show, part Chamber of Commerce claptrap, this fantastic conglomeration was described by
the *Public Ledger* in 1876 when the spontaneous Leicester play
was still being performed.

On New Year's Day the weather was as uncomfortable as usual
lately, but it seemed to have little or no effect on the spirits of
our citizens . . . The Fantasticals or "Shooters" were out in force
during the whole day, and caused much boisterous amusement.
Indians and squaws, princes and princesses, clowns, columbines and
harlequins, negroes of the minstrel-hall type, Chinese and burlesque Dutchmen, bears, apes, and other animals promenaded the
streets to the music of calithumpian cow-bells, or the more digni-
fied brass bands, and kept up their racket until late at night. Inde-
pendence Hall was the grand objective point for them all, and the
old building received many a cheer, both burlesque and serious.
In the middle of the day several of these parties united in one
grand parade and made a striking display.

In 1966, thoroughly televised, it looked like this to scholar
Charles E. Welch, Jr.:

The sound came before the sight—"Oh, Dem Golden Slippers," barely heard, then swelling as thousands of banjos and glockenspiels fed out of the narrow lively streets into Broad Street. They came out of the heart of South Philadelphia then, these unique "Shooters" in their stunning and incongruous magnificence, and the rest of Philadelphia—at least a million and a quarter people —stood to watch them: a Viking carrying a hundred square feet of costume, a Fancy Captain with a train a block long, uncountable clowns in indescribable array, a myriad of musicians—the work of a year expended on one day of glory.

The splendor of the past was lightened by the satire of the present: "General Charles de Gaulle" rested on the seventh day of his labors of creation; "Mary Poppins" drifted above a seamier city than London; "Prince Philip and Princess Margaret" mummed out the fate of modern monarchs; oil lamps were offered neighbors to the north, New York, for subsequent power failures; a Hegeman Bandsman walked in space; American soldiers in Vietnam were warmed by the burning of draft-card burners; the "Great Society" was lampooned by this lesser one. The dead year was held up to a fun house wavy mirror and its events were put in their proper significance of insignificance.

Meanwhile, out in the suburbs, the rest of us "trick or treat for UNICEF," accept a bottle of Beefeater's "Christmas wine" from a customer, and ask Blondie and Dagwood over for cocktails after "the big New Year's game"—stubbornly, with little more on our minds than the "lowest blackguard" of Samuel Breck's Boston.

THE TRIBE OF CHARLES

CHARLES John Huffam Dickens died on June 9, 1870. Legend assures us that a ragamuffin girl hearing the news in Drury Lane raised her troubled eyes and asked, "Dickens dead? Then, will Father Christmas die too?" Her worry inspired Theodore Watts to compose a poetic reply entitled "Dickens Returns on Christmas Day."

> *"Dickens is dead." Beneath that grievous cry*
> *London seemed shivering in the summer heat:*
> *Strangers took up the tale like friends that meet:*
> *"Dickens is dead," said they, and hurried by;*
> *Street children stopped their games—they knew not why,*
> *But some new night seemed darkening down the street;*
> *A girl in rags, staying her way-worn feet,*
> *Cried, "Dickens dead? Will Father Christmas die?"*
> *City he loved, take courage on thy way*
> *He loves thee still in all thy joys and fears:*
> *Though he whose smiles made bright thine eyes of gray—*
> *Whose brave sweet voice, uttering thy tongueless years,*
> *Made laughters bubble through thy sea of tears—*
> *Is gone, Dickens returns on Christmas Day.*

For by the time of his death, Dickens' name had become tightly associated with Christmas on both sides of the Atlantic— Charles Dickens, drummer in a parade of sentimental literature, reviver of "old merry spirit," sometimes called "Father Christmas himself."

The whole thing had started with the chilly reception given the first parts of *Martin Chuzzlewit* early in 1843. *Chuzzlewit*, which began its serialization in January 1843, sold so badly and was reviewed so carpingly that for the first time in his career as a novelist Dickens was "set back." Committed to popular success by his nagging need for money and gnawing social conscience, a frustrated "ham" anyhow, Dickens could not rest on "faint praise" much less failure. Well before *Chuzzlewit* was finished, he "walked . . . 15 and 20 miles about the black streets of London, many and many a night after all sober folks had gone to bed" composing *A Christmas Carol*. The idea for the story is supposed to have come to him as he sat on the platform at a Manchester meeting with Disraeli and other distinguished debaters, and it certainly rose from his convictions that a writer had to keep reaching the widest audience possible in order that edification, education, and reform might take root.

A Christmas Carol tells the story of Ebenezer Scrooge and his conversion. Scrooge is visited one Christmas Eve by the ghost of his old partner, Marley, who has been dead for seven years. Marley upbraids him for his selfishness and narrow ways, telling him to take timely warning. Scrooge then sees the spirits of Christmas Past, Present, and Yet To Come. The spirits all reveal the folly and cruelty of his present self-centered life and show how happy he might be if he opened his heart to others. Scrooge repents and determines to make amends for his past failings. He sends a turkey to the family of his clerk, Bob Cratchit; goes to dinner with his nephew Fred even though he had earlier rejected the invitation; and miraculously becomes "as good a friend, as good a master, and as good a man, as the good old city knew, or any other good old city, town, or borough in the good old world." But one might as well bother, in the words of Dickens' friend and rival William Makepeace Thackeray, "to detail the plot of *The Merry Wives of Windsor,* or *Robinson Crusoe.*"

The *Carol* was published in 1843 in an edition illustrated by Dickens' close friend John Leech of *Punch.* The publication was so lavish and the post-Christmas sales sufficiently mediocre that Dickens realized little immediate financial profit, although the initial edition of 6,000 copies sold out the first day. In fact, coming on the heels of the "failure" of *Martin Chuzzlewit,* the new disappointment caused him to change publishers. However, *A Christmas Carol* gained momentum, and though but 9,000 more copies had been sold by February of 1844, it was receiving enthusiastic applause and had begun its development into a "pop classic," criticism of which (as Coleridge said of Shakespeare) "will alone be genial which is reverential."

Symbolic was the reaction of dour Scottish judge, Francis Jeffrey, who years earlier had helped found and edit the *Edinburgh Review,* that peevish publication with the motto *"judex damnatur, cum nocens absolvitur,"* whose bludgeonings compelled Thomas Moore, for all his endearing young charms, to challenge Jeffrey to a duel and goaded Lord Byron into that outburst entitled "English Bards, and Scotch Reviewers." The editor-judge offered no more perceptive comment than "Blessings on your kind heart, my dear Dickens! and may it always be as light and full as it is kind, and a fountain of kindness to all within reach of its beatings." Jeffrey, who was godfather to Dickens' third son, Francis Jeffrey Dickens, was a "softy" where the younger writer was concerned anyhow. There's a famous story of a good-lady house-guest who found the Judge collapsed in tears over a table in his study. Apologizing for intruding upon his grief, she asked if anyone were dead. "Yes, indeed," replied "the Scotch reviewer," "I'm a great goose to have given away so; but I couldn't help it . . . little Nelly, Boz's little Nelly, is dead!"

Still, it is only with blessings that *A Christmas Carol* can be read. To apply logic to such pieces is not only unfair, but "silly sooth." And logic may well make the reader drop off to sleep reading it—as was the case with Samuel Rogers, a poet who was barely able to complete the copy Dickens sent him. For logic quickly informs us that *A Christmas Carol* is a muddled allegory on the subject of *laissez-faire* economics. Scrooge, grouchy as he may be, is one of many nineteenth-century philistines who pays the exact wages fixed by supply and demand, whose "bah" is no more than an everyday reluctance to be concerned with the plight of the poor, and whose cardinal fault is that he can't be considered a "reasonable" employer. But what "solutions to the Scrooges" are set forth? Cratchit's plight, is worked out "one on one": the employee merely gets a raise quite in line with "reasonable" demand without being offered better opportunities or any basic change in his lot. What, logic asks, about the other unfortunate "cratchits" around town? What has been done about the Ghost's cry, "Mankind was my business. The common welfare was my business: charity, mercy, forbearance, and benevolence . . ."? As R. H. Horne noted in the *Westminster Review* on June (not December) 1844,

. . . [at the end] we might almost suppose the feudal times were returned. The processes whereby poor men are to be enabled to earn good wages, wherewith to buy turkeys for themselves, does not enter into the account; indeed, it would quite spoil the *dé-*

nouement and all the generosity. Who went without turkey and punch in order that Bob Cratchit might get them—for, unless there were turkey and punch in surplus, someone must go without . . . ?

No, *A Christmas Carol* bears analysis little better than the phrase "everybody's beautiful"—but breathes there a man with soul so quick he dares insist so? What Thackeray wrote in *Fraser's Magazine* just a few weeks after publication still holds:

As for the *Christmas Carol,* or any other book of a like nature which the public takes upon itself to criticize, the individual critic had best hold his peace. . . . Who can listen to objections regarding such a book as this? It seems to me a national benefit, and to every man or woman who reads it a personal kindness. The last two people I heard speak of it were women; neither knew the other, or the author, and both said, by way of criticism, "God bless him!" A Scotch philosopher, who nationally does not keep Christmas Day, on reading the book, sent out for a turkey, and asked two friends to dine—this is a fact! Many men were known to sit down after perusing it, and write off letters to their friends, not about business, but out of their fulness of heart, and to wish old acquaintances a happy Christmas. Had the book appeared a fortnight earlier, all the prize cattle would have been gobbled up in pure love and friendship, Epping denuded of sausages, and not a turkey left in Norfolk. . . .

The success of *A Christmas Carol* encouraged Dickens to try again not only in 1844, but in 1845, 1846, and 1848 as well. In *The Chimes* of 1844, he reused the reform motif which had scored twelve months earlier and got an equally good reception. *The Chimes* concerns a ticket porter, Trotty Veck, and his "dream trip" under orders from the Goblin of the Great Bell. Following a small child, the Spirit of Christmas, he is shown the woeful future that awaits the poor, his loved ones, and mankind in general. Awakened by the chiming in of the

New Year, he resolves to apply the lessons of the dream and live with charity in the future. So he does.

This "carol" is much blunter than the first one, scolding the ruling classes because, in Veck's words, "they don't *do* anything for poor people." There is also a good bit of comment on the bourgeois rationalization that the poor keep themselves poor by indifference, laziness, stupid management of their affairs, and incessant breeding. Dickens even toyed with the idea of a "wide awake" tragic ending in which poor, scorned Will Fern, jailed over and over, would finally become a vandal and set fire to the property of the self-centered rich; in which Veck's niece, Lillian, would "go to the streets" and die; and in which his daughter Meg would be overworked into ill-health as her sweetheart, Richard, succumbed to bad companionship and liquor. But he gave in to the romantic nature of the reading public and made the tragedies "dream tragedies," suggesting that the world would not let such awful things happen if it were only made aware that they were happening.

These polemics made the story most controversial, bumping phrases like "this book will melt hearts and open purse strings" against ones like "the poorest production which has yet emanated from his pen" and "one of the most mischievous [books] ever written." *The Chimes* exasperated Dickens' friend Thomas Carlyle, who heard it read and commented,

Dickens is a good little fellow, one of the most cheery, innocent natures I have ever encountered . . . , [but] his theory of life is entirely wrong. He thinks men ought to be buttered up, and the world made soft and accommodating for them, and all sorts of fellows have turkey for their Christmas dinner. Commanding and controlling and punishing he would give up without any misgivings, in order to coax and soothe and delude them into doing right.

The story is not read much any longer, probably because its earnestness strips it of most of its charm. One reviewer in *The Northern Star* commented,

The masses are the victims of undeserved suffering; their cause is a solemn one; and solemnly, with an eloquence that was never excelled; in "thoughts that breathe the words that burn," Mr. Dickens pleads that cause against the cruel, canting, unnatural, blaspheming doctrines and actions of the ruling classes of society.

The Star went on to say, in italics, that *The Chimes* ". . . viewed in its political character and heritage . . . *is decidedly the best work Mr. Dickens has produced.*" But such an observation also points up its weakness as a story to be read year after year by people far less "involved" than Dickens during a season which, good intentions aside, is apt to be more social than socially conscious. For although the Anglo-American twentieth century has embraced "the text" of *The Chimes* quite wholeheartedly, there is an unmerry confusion in that embrace if one has planned to give his wife a stole, his children "wheels," and his dog a steak shortly after reading it.

In spite of the smashing success of *The Cricket on the Hearth* in 1845, Dickens was not up to the inevitable recurrences of the Christmas chore. *Tait's Edinburgh Magazine*, opens its unfavorable review of *The Battle of Life* (a spoonfull of self-abnegation and sentiment offered in 1846) with these remarks:

The Battle of Life is the fourth of Mr. Dickens's annual publications. *The Christmas Carol*, the first and the best, has reached only a *tenth* edition. *The Chimes* was said to be inferior to its predecessor, and is up to the twelfth edition. *The Cricket on the Hearth* had the worst character of the three, and has, therefore, attained its twenty-second edition. The facts merely show that book-buyers and reviewers do not always entertain similar opinions. The latter class

pretty generally asserted that Mr. Dickens was living—so far as his
Annuals were concerned—on his character—eating into his acquired literary capital, while the former has taken care that he
should live upon his edition. No book of the past, or many previous issues, has been so successful as the *Cricket* . . . On the ratio
of increase in the previous publications, the *Battle of Life* will run
into forty-four editions.

Macphail's Edinburgh Ecclesiastical Journal completed what it
had to say about *The Haunted Man* of 1848 by observing: "Let
us have a few more returns of Christmas and Mr. Dickens will
have destroyed his reputation as a tale-writer." Granting that
Christmas books had become a willy-nilly target for the magazine "intellectuals" and that if everybody read the tales every-
other-body abused them, it is still clear that holly-trimmed
charity no longer sparked "Father Christmas's" muse. By the
time Dickens involved himself in the magazines *Household
Words* and *All the Year Round,* "his Christmas stories" were
not about Christmas at all and often not by him either.

One doesn't, however, let the wolves finish off a golden, egg-
laying goose. Dickens had always been a frustrated actor, and
there has been many a learned discussion on this obsession and
the influence of contemporary theater-people like Charles
Matthews and Albert Smith on his novels. It was only natural
with his love of "garish lights," his amateur acting experience,
and his thirst for money, that he would turn to public readings
—and would feature his popular Christmas stories when he did.

Robert Fitzsimons, author of a winsome book about these
entertainments, introduces the study with this paragraph:

The Public Readings of Charles Dickens were the greatest one-
man show of the nineteenth century. "Dickens is coming!" was
the ecstatic shout in towns where he was announced to read. In
London the cheers that greeted his appearance on the platform
could be heard a block away. In Edinburgh he had to calm a

rioting audience. In Glasgow the audience tried to storm the platform and carry him away. In Boston, New York and Philadelphia people queued for tickets all night in temperatures well below freezing point.

And if the adulation was not quite that given Johann Strauss, Benny Goodman, or the Beatles, it was not far less either. For, as Fitzsimons goes on to say, "Dickens was a magnificent actor, with a wonderful talent for mimicry. He seemed able to alter not only his voice, his features and his carriage but also his stature. . . . Character after character appeared on the platform, living and breathing in the flesh."

When he began commercial reading before an audience of 2,000 in Birmingham in December, 1853, he selected *A Christmas Carol* as the vehicle well aware it would take about two hours including a brief intermission. He had tried lengthy Christmas entertainments in private and had had spectacular results. Once, when he read *The Chimes* to the actor William Macready, he reduced the fellow to "undisguisedly sobbing and crying on the sofa." The results at the Birmingham Town Hall were little different. It was an age of emotion, and Victorian audiences were not ashamed to respond. Dickens had them laughing, crying, trembling, exulting—and, like a good actor, he was able to leave them wanting more. They got more too. Two nights later he read *The Cricket on the Hearth* and was persuaded to repeat *A Carol* on the thirtieth, agreeing only when he was assured that working people would be admitted at special prices. A bit cavalierly for a reformer, he reported that the workers ". . . lost nothing, misinterpreted nothing, followed everything closely, laughed and cried with the most delightful earnestness, and animated me to that extent that I felt as if we were all bodily going up into the clouds together."

Later, when he made the exhausting American tour of 1867–

1868, readings of the Christmas stories continued to be a central part of the repertoire. Facing audiences as large as 35,000 people, Dickens drove himself mercilessly as he hurried from engagement to engagement like a dance band barnstorming through the 1930's. He made friends, he made money, he fed his ego, and he ruined his health. Typical was one reading of *A Carol* given in Boston to an audience of close to 10,000. His voice was so tired he could scarcely speak before going on stage; he was so close to nervous exhaustion that he was under a doctor's care two days later; and he was mentally depressed by the side effects of medicines, stimulants, and narcotics. Plans were made to cancel the reading, but Dickens insisted otherwise, saying no performer had a right to break an engagement if he were able to get out of bed. Fitzsimons called this period of Dickens' life "the race"—and "rat-race" it was, if not causing his death, certainly contributing generously to it.

He gave up the platform in 1870 to return to writing. The Final Farewell Reading was given in London melodramatically before 2,034 people, while another 5,000 or so milled about hoping to get in. *A Carol*, along with the trial from *The Pickwich Papers*, were the selections. The reception was appropriately enthusiastic, and when the show was over Dickens spoke a few sentimental words, concluding with his "last goodnight"· " . . . from these garish lights I vanish now forevermore, with a heartfelt, grateful, respectful, affectionate farewell." This was Tuesday, March 15, 1870. Three months later "Father Christmas" was indeed dead.

Dickens was not the first writer to see commercial possibilities in the occasional Christmas story. Prominent among his forerunners was the American Washington Irving—historian, story-teller, essayist, editor, who had so much to do with Saint Nicholas and who at various times in his career was confidant of six presidents and United States Minister to Spain. Irving's versatility resulted in all sorts of observations on "the human comedy," in standard historical studies like the biographies of Columbus and George Washington, in mock treatises like *The Knickerbocker History of New York,* in reports on the Indians, in sketches and short stories. Through them all runs a deep compulsion. Like Ben Franklin before him, he wanted to prove to the world that a man from "the wilderness" could hold his own in wit, in grace, in style with polite Europeans. "Who reads an American book?" queried British critic Sydney Smith. Irving's dream was to hear Europeans reply, "Why, I do!" Ultimately, of course, his dream would be realized, and if more credit has to go to James Fenimore Cooper and the Western writers than to Irving, still "Geoffrey Crayon" and "Diedrich Knickerbocker" did much to open the way.

Irving lived for seventeen years in England. Out of his visit came a series of genial sketches of English country life which proved that a "colonial" could report the foibles and charm of the "old land" as perceptively as Joseph Addison, as happily as Oliver Goldsmith. Most of the material was published in 1819–1820 as *The Sketch-Book of Geoffrey Crayon, Gent.,* along with bric-a-brac like the story about a lazy fellow who went out with his dog Wolf for a walk in the Catskills and fell asleep for twenty years or the one about Brom Bones, the buxom Katrina van Tassel, and a silly schoolmaster named Crane. The last chapter of Volume II centers on a Yuletide visit by Geoffrey Crayon to Bracebridge Hall in Yorkshire. With these pages, Irving not only caught, but pitched, the tone that Dickens and his tribe were to carry down to the very present.

Of all the old festivals, however, that of Christmas awakes the strongest and most heartfelt associations. There is a tone of solemn and sacred feeling that blends with our conviviality, and lifts the spirit to a state of hallowed and elevated enjoyment.

But much of Irving's charm as a writer lies in the fact that he is quizzical and detached even while he is being sentimental. Not one, like Swift, to "hate people" simply because he has seen through them, he loves, like Chaucer, the very foibles he ridicules. The Squire of Bracebridge Hall is an antiquarian: "a strenuous advocate for the revival of old rural games and holiday observances . . . deeply read in the writers, ancient and modern, who have treated on the subject." He has retired to his country estate, trained his family and servants to observe the old ways, celebrate the old festivals, and play the old games "according to their original form." Crayon encounters the son, Frank, by chance and goes with him to spend Christmas at Bracebridge Hall.

As we approached the house, we heard the sound of music, and now and then a burst of laughter, from one end of the building. This, Bracebridge said, must proceed from the servants' hall, where a great deal of revelry was permitted, and even encouraged by the Squire, throughout the twelve days of Christmas, provided everything was done comformably to ancient usage. Here were kept up the old games of hoodman blind, shoe the wild mare, hot cockles, steal the white loaf, bob apple, and snap-dragon; the Yule clog and Christmas candle were regularly burnt, and the mistletoe, with its white berries, hung up, to the imminent peril of all the pretty housemaids.

Christmas breakfast consists of what the Squire "denominates" as "true old English fare."

He indulged in some bitter lamentations over modern breakfasts of tea and toast, which he censured as among the causes of modern effeminacy and weak nerves, and the decline of old English heartiness; and though he admitted them to his table to suit the palates of his guests, yet there was a brave display of cold meats, wine, and ale, on the sideboard. . . . The Squire went on to lament the deplorable decay of the games and amusements which were once prevalent at this season among the lower orders, and countenanced by the higher; when the old halls of the castles and manor-houses were thrown open at daylight; when the tables were covered with brawn, and beef, and humming ale; when the harp and the carol resounded all day long, and when rich and poor were alike welcome to enter and make merry. "Our old games and local customs," said he, "had a great effect in making the peasant fond of his home, and the promotion of them by the gentry made him fond of his lord. They made the times merrier, and kinder, and better, and I can truly say, with one of our old poets,—

*'I like them well—the curious preciseness,
And all-pretended gravity of those
That seek to banish hence these harmless sports
Have thrust away much ancient honesty.'*

"The nation," continued he, "is altered; we have almost lost our simple true-hearted peasantry. They have broken asunder from the higher classes, and seem to think their interests are separate. They have become too knowing, and begin to read newspapers, listen to ale-house politicians, and talk of reform. I think one mode to keep them in good-humor in these hard times would be for the nobility and gentry to pass more time on their estates, mingle more among the country people, and set the merry old English games going again."

Such was the good Squire's project for mitigating public discontent: and, indeed, he had once attempted to put his doctrine in practice, and a few years before had kept open house during the holidays in the old style. The country people, however, did not understand how to play their parts in the scene of hospitality; many uncouth circumstances occurred; the manor was overrun by all the vagrants of the country, and more beggars drawn into the neighborhood in one week than the parish officers could get rid of in a year. Since then, he had contented himself with inviting the decent part of the neighboring peasantry to call at the hall on Christmas day, and with distributing beef, and bread, and ale, among the poor, that they might make merry in their own dwellings.

Exactly how influential Irving was on Dickens is a matter of some dispute, but the two men were acquainted, read each other, and held each other in high respect. Irving was instrumental in getting Dickens to come to America for the first time, complimenting him on *The Old Curiosity Shop* and beginning a mutual admiration correspondence. At the dinner of welcome in New York City in 1842, Irving, then fifty-nine years old, was in the chair, and when Dickens addressed the 800 diners, he paid the following compliment:

"Washington Irving! Why, gentlemen, I don't go upstairs to bed two nights out of the seven . . . without taking Washington Irving under my arm; and when I don't take him, I take his own brother, Oliver Goldsmith. . . . Washington Irving—Diedrich Knickerbocker—Geoffrey Crayon—why, where can you go that they have not been there before? Is there an English farm—is there an English stream, an English city, or an English country-seat, where they have not been? Is there no Bracebridge Hall in existence? Has it no ancient shades or quiet streets?"

Irving was so moved, he broke down in replying. Never much for speaking anyhow, he was "terrified" he would be unable to "get through" this particular occasion. After Dickens speech he rose, received long and deafening applause, and began to talk. He got through two or three sentences when his voice cracked. He tried to maintain control, but finally gave up, made a couple of offhand remarks, and sat down after a simple toast to "Charles Dickens, the guest of the nation." "There," he is supposed to have remarked, "there, I told you I should break down, and I've done it."

After the dinner, the two men journeyed to Washington, spent a few days together, and parted literally "in sadness and tears." Shortly, Dickens wrote these words to Irving: "Wherever you go, God bless you! What pleasure I have had in seeing and

talking with you, I will not attempt to say. I shall never forget it as long as I live." Influences, especially subtle influences
of one writer on another, are nearly impossible to caliper; but
it is hard to believe that Dickens didn't have Bracebridge Hall
somewhere in mind—if not each time he undertook his December task, at least when Mr. Pickwick went to Dingley Dell.

But the little girl in Drury Lane need not have looked wor-
ried, even with both Irving and Dickens dead. Dickens' speaking tours had started a parade of openly sentimental Christmas
writing in which almost anyone could march. Kate Douglas
Wiggin twirled a baton. A kindergarten teacher, who wrote
Rebecca of Sunnybrook Farm and *Mother Carey's Chickens*,
she had met Dickens in 1868 on a train between Boston and
Portland, Maine, when she was only a child and he was "the
famous lecturer." She recognized him on the platform, boldly
contrived to sit next to him, and told him how she had read
David Copperfield six times even though there were some "dull
passages" that she disliked. He put his arm about her and held
her hand as they talked of dogs, reading, and the personalities
Dickens had created. Dickens, she claims, told her he cried
when he wrote *A Christmas Carol* and whenever he read it
in public.

Nearly twenty years later, Kate Wiggin wrote her own Christmas story. It was a tale of a lame girl born on Christmas Day and
named Carol by her parents, Mr. and Mrs. Bird. *The Birds'
Christmas Carol* was privately printed in San Francisco in 1886,
bound in paper covers, and sold for the benefit of the Silver
Street Kindergarten, where Kate Wiggin taught. Finally, a copy
was sent to Henry O. Houghton of Houghton Mifflin Co., who
read it to his family on a summer day and said he was going to
get it published whether his associates liked it or not. They did
like it, and so did everyone else. *The Birds' Christmas Carol* was

a great success, translated into several foreign languages, into Braille, and eventually made into a play, for many years as popular as anything the "genial" man on the train with "the red carnation in the buttonhole" had ever done.

However, Bret Harte, not Kate Wiggin, is called "The American Dickens" by those who indulge in epithets. Harte did read a lot of Dickens and was heavily influenced by him. In fact, just before the Englishman died, he wrote to his "New California" counterpart asking him to do a story for *All the Year Round*. Both writers are similar in their uses of open sentimentality, melodrama, and story matter tailored to meet the tastes of "the everyday young man." But close grouping is unfair to Dickens, whose sincerity, genius, and scope are belittled in comparison to an opportunist once described by Mark Twain as having a pump where his heart should be. In Christmas matters, if we must have an "American Dickens," William Sidney Porter (O. Henry) should be the choice—not because he aped Dickens, for he didn't, but because his is the name that will be uttered if you stop someone on the street and say what American writer do you think of when I say "Christmas"?

O. Henry's reputation rests on two stories that are still "pop classics" in this country—if not as widely read, recited, and adapted as *A Christmas Carol*, certainly "outselling" *The Chimes* and *The Cricket on the Hearth*. They are *The Gift of the Magi* and *The Cop and the Anthem*. Both are out-and-out tearjerkers, combining the sentimentality of the season with Porter's patented, and sardonic, "trick ending." The first tells of the poor boy who sells his treasured family watch that he may give his poor wife Christmas combs for her lovely, long hair at the same time the wife is having her hair cut that she may buy a watch-chain for her husband. The other tells of a bum who tries to commit his annual crime so he can spend the cold months in a warm cell. As it is Christmas Eve, no one will arrest him. Listening to an anthem, he sees himself for what he is and decides to reform—only to be picked up for loitering. Porter, whom most people recall as an ex-jailbird and alcoholic newsman, had his fingers right where the American pulse beats, and these two stories are sure to come out with the baubles and tinsel as long as there are philistines to "jostle."

Actually the tale that has grown up around *The Gift of the Magi* makes a pretty good Christmas story in itself. The legend is recorded by Robert H. Davis and Arthur B. Maurice in their biography, *The Caliph of Bagdad*. You can believe it or not, according to how many lumps you like in your tea. The scene is New York City in late November 1905. For three years, Porter has been a successful writer for the *World*. The editor has asked him for a story to go in the magazine section of the Christmas number. It will be illustrated in color by Dan Smith, the paper's top artist. Smith is anxious to get started, but, per usual, there has been no word about the story from O. Henry. So Smith goes to Porter's rooms at 55 Irving Place, where he not only discovers the author, but also the fact that nothing has been done about the story. "I must get to work at once," Smith growls. "Can't you tell me something to draw and then fit your story to it?" For a time O. Henry is quiet, then he says: "I'll tell you what to do, Colonel. Just draw a picture of a poorly finished room, the kind you find in a boarding house or rooming house over on the West Side. In the room there is only a chair or two, a chest of drawers, a bed, and a trunk. On the bed a man and a girl are sitting side by side. They are talking about Christmas. The man has a watch fob in his hand. He is playing with it while he is thinking. The girl's principal feature is the long, beautiful hair that is hanging down her back. That is all I can think of now. But the story is coming."

When Smith leaves, Porter, with characteristic singleness of purpose, begins to work on an entirely different story. Soon, however, he gets back on the track. He calls a friend, Lindsey Denison, and tells him to come over. "I've got to forget the story I'm working on," he says, "and write another one. Have to have it done this afternoon and not a line written. I've thought of an idea for it, but I need a living model. You are that model. I'm going to write a story about you and your wife. I've never met your wife, but I think you two are the kind that would make sacrifices for each other. Now stay on the sofa and don't interrupt." Three hours later "The Gift of the Magi" is ready for the press, the girl with the lovely hair and the sweet nature a picture not of Denison's wife but of Porter's first wife, Athol Estes, who had sent him Christmas boxes when he was "exiled" in Honduras, who "had a habit of saying little silent prayers about the simplest everyday thing," and who had died eight years earlier.

But the "Tribe of Charles" as the merchants of Christmas writing might be called is large. Beyond the obvious professionalisms of Wiggin, Harte, and Porter lie a thousand "tours sans force" essayed in a hundred thousand magazines, journals, and newpapers by hacks who capitalize on the good will of editors toward anything Christmas. Perhaps the *Stock Growers' Journal* of Miles City, Montana, isn't the typical American publication, but its pages of 1893 do mark the literary level of what is printed during December out where "the dark fields of the republic" roll on "under the night." Besides social notes which observe that twenty "tinhorn gamblers" are in for a rough holiday because the chief of police has told them to leave town "or else" and which go on to state that the editorial offices will be open on Christmas Day to receive delinquent subscriptions, the *Journal* features an appropriate poem. The choice for '93

was "A Busted Cowboy's Christmas" by Iyam B. Usted, probably D. J. O'Malley, who wrote "When the Work's All Done
This Fall."

> I am a busted cowboy
>   And I work upon the range;
> In Summer time I get some work
>   But one thing that is strange,
> As soon as Fall work's over
>   We get it in the neck
> And we get a Christmas present
>   On a neatly written check.
>
> Then come to town to rusticate,
>   We've no place else to stay
> When Winter winds are howling
>   Because we can't eat hay.
> A puncher's life's a picnic;
>   It is one continued joke,
> But there's none more anxious to see Spring
>   Than a cowboy who is broke.
>
> The wages that a cowboy earns
>   In Summer go like smoke,
> And when the Winter snows have come
>   You bet your life he's broke.
> You can talk about your holiday,
>   Your Christmas cheer and joy;
> It's all the same to me, my friend,
>   Cash gone—I'm a broke cowboy.
>
> My saddle and my gun's in soak,
>   My spurs I've long since sold;
> My rawhide and my quirt are gone;
>   My chaps—no, they're too old;
> My stuff's all gone, I can't even beg
>   A solitary smoke.

> *For no one cares what becomes of*
> *A cowboy who is broke.*
>
> *Now, where I'll eat my dinner*
> *This Christmas, I don't know;*
> *But you bet I'm going to have one*
> *If they give me half a show.*
> *This Christmas has no charms for me,*
> *On good things I'll not choke,*
> *Unless I get a big hand-out—*
> *I'm a cowboy who is broke.*

Clearly, anything that smacks of December 25 will do. Even so, matters are extreme when a reputable magazine like *Yankee* burdens its pages with material as nondescript as this entry for Captain George Blunt Wendell's logbook aboard the *Galatea* (out of Boston, bound for Manila) in 1862—

Christmas Day, Dec. 25—Comes in with light westerly winds and broken clouds, with some N.E. swell. All hands work scrubbing between decks. During the night light airs and calms . . . a finback whale gamboling alongside. . . . Pumps attended. Ship making no water. Carpenter putting in chain box. . . . Oh, my precious wife that I could be with thee and our darling daughter. It makes me real homesick to think of it. . . . For both, I am all thine own and ever love . . .

—particularly when Christmas was such an insignificant day in the maritime world of the nineteenth century. Joseph Conrad, for one, notes in his *Tales of Hearsay, and Last Essays* that in "20 years of wandering over the restless waters of the globe" he can recall but one Christmas Day celebrated by a present given and received. That was the exchange of a keg of provisions, a bundle of newspapers, and two boxes of figs between an English "wool clipper" and a Yankee whaler in the Southern Ocean in 1879. He concludes his description by remarking that except on passenger ships "Christmas Days at sea are of varied character, fair to middling and down to plainly atrocious."

But to return to the professionals, "fair to middling and down to plainly atrocious" isn't an unjust evaluation of most all the work that emerges from this business of

> *Robbers do not rob the town*
> *And atheists take* Bibles *down,*
> *At Christmas time.*

For if the literary critics have taken Thackeray's advice and held their peace on the subject, the fact remains Christmas has done little to inspire important creative work. Nor is the reason hard to come by. Poor, mediocre, commercial writing is much like advertising in that the authors study their public, comprehend what that public wants, and go about offering it to them. The formula is to curry already established attitudes and sentiments like a Marxist who will yell "Down with Capitalism!" at a Communist rally and then basks in the *olés*. Great writers don't do this sort of thing easily. Their genius compels them to record life as it looks to them, not as others would have it. The conventionality of Christmas, alone, not only stultifies, but even confounds, such genius—as surely as it panders to mediocrity.

Should one who knows great writing "suspend his Christian spirit" and in the "dog days of August" take down an anthology like William K. Seymour and John Smith's *Happy Christmas* or Daniel J. Foley's *Christmas in the Good Old Days,* he will cough, appalled at the quality of the selections. Out of his study will echo "bah" upon "humbug" as he notes the list of distinguished authors (William Dean Howells, Robert Herrick, Sarah Orne Jewett, William Carlos Williams, Dylan Thomas, George Eliot, etc., etc.), all trapped like flies in fudge, struggling wearily to free their muses from the firmly established sentimental characterization, sentimental setting, sentimental action, even sentimental style ordered by the occasion. Where literature is really taken to task, *comme ci, comme ça,* by students, scholars, and critics, in the college and graduate school courses, one might easily obtain his Ph.D. and find it hard to recall any Christmas story or Christmas poem other than Milton's "On the Morning of Christ's Nativity," which he encountered *en route.* And this is not because the learned are misanthropes. The scholar buys his mother a rocking chair with shawl, reads his kiddies *How the Grinch Stole Christmas,* and waters the poinsettia with "the whole world and his aunt." It's just that business and sentiment mix no better in the seminar than they do in the Internal Revenue Service.

Predictably, truly great Christmas writing has occurred most often when the subject has been approached obliquely, when the author was on the scent of some other matter and simply ran by Christmas nearly unawares. Were some heathen to stop me in the stacks asking what writers he might read to learn about Christmas as it really is, not as it is meant to be, I could do a lot worse than send him to the folklore surveyed in the earlier chapters. But if he insisted, wanted to read "polite literature" not folklore, I would not send him to Dickens or Wiggin or O. Henry. I'd give him call letters that would lead to passages such as the opening section of Thomas Hardy's *Under the Greenwood Tree;* to Chapter 22 of Herman Melville's *Moby Dick;* to the winter stanzas in Alfred, Lord Tennyson's *In Memoriam;* and to Robert Southwell's poem, "The Burning Babe." There is no equivocation in these four vignettes. They ring true to the "walking shadows" who strut, and briefly fret their Christmas quotas year by year. To their music, let me "drown my book."

Thomas Hardy was a realist and, as we have seen, a student of folkways. He has few illusions about the creatures who people his books. Like most men when confronted by tradition, his West Country villagers celebrate the Christmas season the way swallows return to Capistrano, regularly, stolidly, moved by "inner compulsions." They neither enjoy nor dislike the act of caroling they perform as the book opens. But they cannot omit it, just as their ancestors could not omit it and, they trust, their generation will not be able to omit it.

"Number seventy-eight," he softly gave out as they formed round in a semicircle, the boys opening the lanterns to get clearer light, and directing their rays on the books.

Then passed forth into the quiet night an ancient and well-worn hymn, embodying Christianity in words peculiarly befitting the simple and honest hearts of the quaint characters who sang them so earnestly.

> *"Remember Adam's fall*
> *O thou man. . . ."*

Melville recognized this facet of Christmas "celebration" too. His Quakers work the day, embarking from the warmth and security of Nantucket Harbor to plunge blindly "like fate into the lone Atlantic." Symbolically, they have left the warmth and security of disciplined Christianity to follow after a mad Captain on a personal, philosophic quest against Evil in the form of a white whale. "Wanderers on the restless waters of the globe," like Conrad they are barely aware of Christmas—hoping, not trusting, there truly is a Saviour and "a triumph of the skies."

At last the anchor was up, the sails were set, and off we glided. It was a short, cold Christmas; and as the short northern day merged into night, we found ourselves almost broad upon the wintry ocean, whose freezing spray cased us in ice, as in polished armor. The long rows of teeth on the bulwarks glistened in the moonlight; and like the white ivory tusks of some huge elephant, vast curving icicles depended from the bows.

Lank Bildad, as pilot, headed the first watch, and ever and anon, as the old craft deep dived into the green seas, and sent the shivering frost all over her, and the winds howled, and the cordage rang, his steady notes were heard,—

> *"Sweet fields beyond the swelling flood,*
> *Stand dressed in living green.*
> *So to the Jew old Canaan stood,*
> *While Jordan rolled between."*

Never did those sweet words sound more sweetly to me than then. They were full of hope and fruition. Spite of this frigid winter night in the boisterous Atlantic, spite of my wet feet and wetter jacket, there was yet, it then seemed to me, many a pleasant haven in store; and meads and glades so eternally vernal, that the grass shot up by the spring, untrodden, unwilted, remains at mid-summer.

But for Alfred, Lord Tennyson, Christmas was a personal, poignant day. On September 15, 1833, his closest friend, Arthur Henry Hallam had died suddenly of "apoplexy" within "Vienna's fatal walls." Hallam, who had gone to Cambridge with Tennyson and who had been engaged to marry Tennyson's sister Emily, was on a European tour with his distinguished father, historian Henry Hallam. The death, and its suddenness, stunned the poet who subsequently passed through a long period of religious agony. *In Memoriam* is the record of this questioning, of the doubt that a benevolent God could allow those whom He clearly loves to die so young. It was composed over seventeen years and is the statement of "a man solitary and sad, carrying a bit of Chaos about him."

Symbols of conventional faith, the Christmases of 1833, 1834, and 1837 divide the poem and Tennyson's grief—first measur-

ing how long since the poet has heard "the sound of a voice that
is still" and "felt the touch of a vanish'd hand":

XXVIII (1833)

The time draws near the birth of Christ:
The moon is hid; the night is still;
The Christmas bells from hill to hill
Answer each other in the mist.

Four voices of four hamlets round,
From far and near, on mead and moor,
Swell out, and fail, as if a door
Were shut between me and the sound:

Each voice four changes on the wind,
That now dilate, and now decrease,
Peace and goodwill, goodwill and peace,
Peace and goodwill, to all mankind.

This year I slept and woke with pain,
I almost wished no more to wake,
And that my hold on life would break
Before I heard those bells again:

But they my troubled spirit rule,
For they controlled me when a boy;
They bring me sorrow touched with joy,
The merry merry bells of Yule.

—then measuring how sorrow numbs and changes:

LXXVIII (1834)

Again at Christmas did we weave
The holly round the Christmas hearth;

The silent snow possessed the earth,
And calmly fell our Christmas Eve:

The yule-clog sparkled keen with frost,
No wing of wind the region swept,
But over all things brooding slept
The quiet sense of something lost.

As in the winters left behind,
Again our ancient games had place,
The mimic picture's breathing grace,
And dance and song and hoodman-blind.

Who showed a token of distress?
No single tear, no mark of pain:
O sorrow, then can sorrow wane?
O grief, can grief be changed to less?

O last regret, regret can die!
No—mixed with all this mystic frame,
Her deep relations are the same,
But with long use her tears are dry.

In Memoriam ends with religious reconciliation and "happiness," and with Tennyson's "conviction that fear, doubts, and suffering will find answer to relief only through Faith in a God of Love." The Christmas of 1837 arrives and goes.

CIV (1837)

The time draws near the birth of Christ;
The moon is hid, the night is still;
A single church below the hill
Is pealing, folded in the mist.

A single peal of bells below,
That wakens at this hour of rest

A single murmur in the breast,
That these are not the bells I know.

Like strangers' voices here they sound,
In lands where not a memory strays,
Nor landmark breathes of other days,
But all is new unhallowed ground.

—and the description ends with the "wild bells" ringing out "the grief that saps the mind," ringing in a "Christ that is to be."

Jesuit Robert Southwell had, of course, few doubts—his faith so ardent that he died for it on February 21, 1595 in Protestant England, imprisoned for three years, tortured, hanged at thirty-four like the common criminal upon a "Tyburn tree." His dead body was quartered and drawn. Southwell had been the spiritual advisor to Anne Howard and her recusant husband, the Earl of Arundel. His time at Arundel House in London was full of narrow escapes from sadistic Richard Topcliffe and the Protestant "pursuivants" interspersed with long periods of tedious concealment. During these days he wrote steadily, publishing poems and tracts through a secret Roman Catholic press. The output reflects the ardent piety of a man who frequently stole outside the city to succor Catholic families and who was ultimately arrested while celebrating Mass in a Catholic household near Harrow.

THE BURNING BABE

As I in hoary winter's night stood shivering in the snow,
Surprised I was with sudden heat which made my heart to glow;
And lifting up a fearful eye to view what fire was near,
A pretty babe, all burning bright, did in the air appear,
Who, scorchèd with excessive heat, such floods of tears did shed,
As though his floods should quench his flames which with his tears
   were fed;

"Alas!" quoth he, "but newly born in fiery heats I fry,
Yet none approach to warm their hearts or feel my fire but I!

My faultless breast the furnace is, the fuel, wounding thorns;
Love is the fire and sighs the smoke, the ashes, shame and scorns;
The fuel Justice layeth on, and Mercy blows the coals;
The metals in this furnace wrought are men's defilèd souls;
For which, as now on fire I am to work them to their good,
So will I melt into a bath to wash them in my blood."
With this he vanished out of sight, and swiftly shrunk away,
And straight I callèd unto mind that it was Christmas-day.

Wessex caroler, Quaker whaler, Cambridge Apostle, London martyr—perhaps any art burns down to the response Christina Rossetti once gave:

> *What can I give Him*
> *Poor as I am?*
> *If I were a shepherd*
> *I would bring a lamb,*
> *If I were a wise man*
> *I would do my part—*
> *Yet what can I give Him?*
> *Give my heart.*

That, so be it, is the most we can ask of any Milton, glorious or inglorious, wherever or when.

INDEXES

Persons (includes legendary and mythological figures):

Hadman, John: 134
Hall, Edward: 9
Hallam, Arthur H.: 177
Hallam, Henry: 177
Halpert, Herbert: 35
Hamilton, Alexander: 87
Handel, George Frederick: 109, 110, 114
Hardy, Thomas: 41, 143–146, 175, 176, 181
Harper, Fletcher: 92
Harte, Bret: 93, 169, 171
Hatcher, John: 75
Hawthorne, Nathaniel: 19
Haydn, Franz Joseph: 109
Helen of Mecklenburg: 19
Henry V (of England): 139
Henry VI (of England): 120
Henry VIII (of England): 9, 63, 73, 132
Hercules: 50
Herod: 46f., 72, 109f.
Herrick, Robert: 31–32, 174
Hiawatha: 110
Hill, Richard: 108
Holley, Orville L.: 87–88
Hone, P.: 88
Hone, William: 133
Horne, R. H.: 157
Horner, Thomas: 63
Horsley, J. C.: 38
Houghton, Henry O.: 168
Howard, Anne: 180
Howells, William Dean: 174

Irving, Washington: 17, 84f., 163–168

Jason: 50
Jeffrey, Francis: 156–157
Jesus Christ (Life and Legend): 5,
47–73, 81f., 96, 115–131
Jewett, Sarah Orne: 174
Jocapone, da Todi: 101, 114
Jones, Charles W.: 81, 85
Jonson, Ben:
    Christmas His Masque: 10–11
    Volpone: 123
Joseph (*See* St. Joseph)
Joseph of Arimathea: 58–63, 118
Josephes: 60
Judas: 49–51, 53f.
Justinian: 5, 80

Keats, John: 21, 44
Kelly, W.: 140–143
Knecht Ruprecht: 83, 96
Knox, John: 14
Kriss Kringle: 84, 92

Lee, Brenda: 114
Leech, John: 156
Lewis, C. S.: 48
Lewis, Lionel S.: 62
Libanius: 4
Livingston, Henry, Jr.: 88–90
Longfellow, Henry Wadsworth: 110
Loomis, Roger: 59–60
Luther, Martin: 8, 19, 107, 110
Lyon, Mary: 15

Macready, William: 162
Marks, Johnny: 95
Mary (*See* St. Mary)
Mary (of England): 8, 38
Mary Magdalene: 50, 117
Mason, Lowell: 110
Mather, Cotton: 107
Mather, Increase: 107
Matthews, Charles: 161
Maurice, Arthur B.: 170
May, Robert L.: 95

PLACES AND SUBJECTS:

Titles, and Long Quotations from Songs, Rhymes, Tales, Poems